Candy Girl

HOW I GAVE UP SUGAR AND BUILT A SWEETER LIFE BETWEEN MEALS

Copyright © 2016 by Jill Kelly

All rights reserved. No part of this book may be used or reproduced by any means, graphic, electronic, mechanical, or digital, including photocopying, recording, taping, or by any information storage retrieval system without the express written permission of the author except in the case of brief quotations embodied in critical articles and reviews.

Cover and book design by
Amy Livingstone, Sacred Art Studio,
sacredartstudio.net

ISBN-13:978-1539392064
(3 Cats Publishing)

ISBN-10:1539392066

Candy Girl

HOW I GAVE UP SUGAR
AND BUILT A SWEETER
LIFE BETWEEN MEALS

Jill Kelly, PhD

ALSO BY JILL KELLY

Sober Truths: The Making of an Honest Woman

Sober Play: Using Creativity for a More Joyful Recovery

Fiction
The Color of Longing
Fog of Dead Souls
When Your Mother Doesn't
Broken Boys
That Night in the Apartment

For all the girls and boys and women and men
who use sugar and food to make their pain go away

Foreword

Last week I called up my old lover Sugah. You know how when you come back into town after being gone a long time and you just can't keep yourself from driving by his house, you know, just to take the trip down Memory Lane, and just by chance he's home and the lights are on and you think, wow, it can't hurt to just stop by and say hello. It's been a long time and he's not going to be interested in you (he's probably taken up with someone else by now) and you know you're not going to be interested in him because you're married to Healthy Eating now and you just know you won't break that commitment.

But Sugah invites you in and he's really glad to see you. He's watching reruns of West Wing *with your mutual friend Cheetos, and Cheetos pulls you down to sit right between them and they wrap their arms around you and those old seductive feelings start up and you think, wow, I can stay here for a day or two. Hell, it's the holidays and everybody I know is coming over to the party and I can leave anytime I want to.*

After a couple of days, Cheetos leaves and you're glad to see him go because your mouth hurts after he kisses you and your fingers turn orange from touching him, but Sugah is so sweet to you and he makes all the old promises and you think about leaving but it's so much easier to hang out there because your anxiety goes away and your burden of responsibility is buried under a few dozen wrappers. And then you can't quite zip your pants and nothing real tastes very good anymore and Sugah wants to spend all day watching Netflix and you need to go to work and he promises to come by on your breaks and he does and then he's waiting when you get home and it seems all okay and then it doesn't.

And so you bite the bullet and stop buying more tickets for the merry-go-round because it wasn't all that merry and you just hope Healthy Eating is waiting up and will take you back when you drag your sorry ass through the door.

IT'S NOT TOO LATE

Chances are that if you're reading this book, you're not 15. Or even 25 or 35. If you are that young, you're probably looking for another diet or hoping that I've got the miracle answer for how you can eat all you want and not gain weight or have health issues. When you've been to the refrigerator a few million times like I have, you've figured out that that isn't going to happen. Oh, we go on hoping but we know it isn't true. There are only a couple of answers that work: eat the right foods and not too much of them, exercise steadily and wisely, and, perhaps most importantly, heal your emotional wounds.

I'm 69 years old. I've been up and down the scale for the last 25 years, mostly up. And I have learned to eat moderately and exercise moderately and I can keep my weight at a much more comfortable place but only if I don't eat sugar. When I eat sugar, I binge on candy, ice cream, and other sweets and then somehow, some way, I slip into a space of WHY THE HELL NOT, and I eat everything I want: grilled cheese sandwiches, fish and chips, hot buttered naan, doughnuts, you name it. I throw off what feel like the shackles of abstinence and go hog wild. My dormant fat cells have a field day, and then in a few months the 30 lost pounds are 40 gained.

To be honest, I've been tempted to give up, to just be a fat old person. But I don't want to be a fat old person. It isn't the vanity of my earlier years that's calling to me anymore. It's the bad back, the threat of heart disease and diabetes. It's the difficulty of tying my shoes or clipping my toenails. I don't want to be incapacitated. Trekking in Nepal is not on my bucket list, but sitting comfortably in any movie theater or airplane seat is.

So one of my intentions is to preach the message that it's not too late. Whatever your age, whatever my age, it is not too late.

I hope the ideas and suggestions and questions in this book will give you the courage to make the changes that you need. And let's face it. I want this book to keep me inspired too. I want to write my way into lasting recovery from sugar and food addiction.

HOWEVER, IT SEEMS ONLY FAIR TO WARN YOU…

This book does not contain any magic solutions to the addiction to sugar and the obsession with food. If you're anything like me, you've spent a lot of time and money looking for that magic. You've suffered through diet after diet always to end up in the same place or worse. Although we don't want to believe it, and we may keep searching, we know that the quick fixes don't work and that the simple pill or mantra doesn't exist. But there is hope. And it doesn't take starvation or eating the same thing all the time or being miserable. It doesn't take seaweed wraps at a spa or six hours a day of exercise.

It may take a certain level of misery though, misery and desperation. It did for me. I had to get miserably obese, desperately tired of the merry-go-round of slow weight loss and fast weight gain and more and more limitations.

But it also takes some very good things, things you already have but may not have considered as allies and gifts in this struggle: your acceptance, your courage, your persistence, your sense of humor, and your ability to change your story. Here's how I changed my story and some ideas for how you can change yours.

A WORD ABOUT SUGAR ADDICTION AND ALCOHOLISM

I've been self-medicating with sugar and food for most of my life. For 20 years in the middle, alcohol was my primary addiction. I didn't know for a long time that the two problems are the same problem for me. But when I got sober in 1989, sugar again became my poison of choice. If you are an alcoholic who suffers from sugar and food addiction as I do, this book is for you. If you are not an alcoholic but you suffer from sugar and food addiction, this book is also for you.

When we talk to recovering alcoholics and addicts, we find a very common refrain: I started using sugar or food just like I was using alcohol.

— Phil Werdell, co-founder of ACORN
Food Dependency Recovery Services

A WORD ABOUT ANOREXIA AND BULIMIA

Anorexia and bulimia have not been part of my path, so this book doesn't address those relationships with food. My eating disorders are on the other end of the spectrum: compulsive overeating and weight gain. However, all of us who struggle with food share many of the same difficulties. We all seek to find peace with food and to do that, I believe we need to create engaging and fulfilling lives between meals. Much of what I've written here may resonate with you even if the way we eat doesn't look the same.

HOW TO USE THIS BOOK

I wrote this book to record my experience, strength, and hope around recovering from food addiction. Part memoir, part how-to, part ruminations and understandings, the book is loosely organized in sections of what it was like for me, what happened, what it's like now, and the tools I am using to deepen my recovery and prevent relapse.

You can read this book in the usual way: starting at the beginning and reading through to the end. Alternately you can use it as a meditation/journaling guide, using the 210 list in the back to find discussions relevant to your current circumstances. And then again, you can just dip in and out as you need it.

The Food for Thought questions in each section are great for daily journaling or for discussion with your recovery buddy or small group. I use them regularly in my own recovery. Note that you don't need a new special notebook or journal for this. Use one of the many you've already written three pages in. You can also post your responses and questions on the program's Facebook page @lifebetweenmeals.

The Tools for Change can help you get started. Other tools are available at **www.lifebetweenmealscoaching.com**.

I am so glad you are curious about creating a life between meals. It's given me a way out and I hope you will find that it does that for you too.

Table of Contents

PART I: THE WAY IN 1

How I fell into sugar and food addiction 2
Is sugar addiction real? 29
Breaking free 40
The obstacles to overcome 52
How soothing ourselves is the real problem 80

PART II: THE WAY OUT 101

Changing our stories 102
Growing up 114
Changing our brains 120
Managing our stresses 141
Abstinence in one form or another 165
Changing our lives 176
Changing our relationship with food 194
Changing our relationship with ourselves 220
We can't go it alone 253
Tools we can use to support our recovery 263
Using creativity for a stronger recovery 283
Other ways of taking care of ourselves 290
Being in recovery for the long haul 298
Creating the life between meals 318
I know you can do it 331

RESOURCES 345

THE LIFE BETWEEN MEALS PROGRAM 347

CONNECTING WITH THE AUTHOR 349

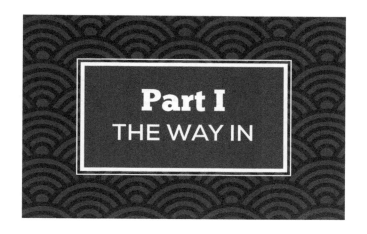

Part I
THE WAY IN

HOW I FELL INTO SUGAR AND FOOD ADDICTION

1
I'M ADDICTED TO SUGAR

The word *addicted* gets thrown around a lot. "I'm addicted to *House of Cards* or *Dancing with the Stars*. I'm addicted to the Harry Potter books. I'm addicted to the French fries at Big Al's Burgers." This is meant to be cute.

But my sugar addiction isn't cute and its impact isn't benign. It's done a very negative number on my blood pressure and my cholesterol levels. It has put hundreds of pounds on my body. It has mired me in guilt, shame, self-loathing, and a myriad of other emotional miseries.

So why don't I leave it alone? Because I can't. I can't take it or leave it. If I take it, I can't leave it. It's a simple truth but a very hard one to live with.

Addiction is often characterized as an allergy in the body (an unhealthy response) and an obsession in the mind. Neither of these is cute.

I am also an alcoholic. In my case, this is not a coincidence, for alcohol in its many forms is just fermented sugars. Same allergy, same kind of obsession. Same misery. Not every sugar addict is an alcoholic and not every alcoholic is a sugar addict, but many of us are even if we don't know it or want to know it.

It isn't cute to be a food addict. It isn't romantic or dramatic either. There are some great movies about alcoholics and drug addicts, from *The Lost Weekend* to *Leaving Las Vegas*, from *I'm Dancing as Fast as I Can* to *Clean and Sober* to *When a Man Loves a Woman*. But nobody makes movies about food addicts, too much misery, too little sensationalism.

Food addiction is a crippling drudgery. If you have it, you know what I'm talking about. I didn't expect to have it. I fought the idea that I have it for decades. Now I accept that this is part of my journey. If it's part of yours, read on.

2
THREE EXPERIENCES THAT SET ME UP FOR SELF-MEDICATING WITH FOOD

Before the age of 9, I have no memories that involve food. I have memories of school, of my parents, of my siblings, of moving from Portland to Denver, of rooms and yards and trips. But no memories of food.

Then when I was 9, three experiences changed me and I stepped into a world of hurt that needed soothing.

Experience #1

On a sunny afternoon in the fall of 1956, I was outside playing with my sisters, age 6 and 2. I had turned over my bike and was clipping playing cards onto the spokes so they would make that lovely clickety-clack when I ride. My youngest sister, Kerry, was turning the pedals and watching the gears go around. Somehow I stopped paying attention to her and moved away or turned away, and she stuck her fingers into the gears. There was blood and her howling face. Soon we were all screaming and my parents came running. They read me the riot act for being careless, snatched up Kerry, and went off to the hospital, leaving me awash in guilt and shame. If they spoke to me about it more reasonably when they returned, I don't remember. I know now they were terrified and that they thrust that fear onto me. That didn't help me at the time. At the time, I felt wrong, so wrong, useless, irresponsible, dangerous. At the time, I started turning to food to soothe my emotions.

Experience #2

When we'd lived only eight months in Colorado, my dad lost his new job and we moved back to the Pacific Northwest. While my folks waited for the Colorado house to sell, we stayed with my father's parents, who were caretakers on a big rambling summer estate along the Columbia River. Their home was a 3-room apartment above the garage with a bedroom for them and a couch for my mother and the baby. My brother and sister and I had to sleep across the road in what was called "the Big House," where the owners stayed when they came up each summer. Now it was shuttered for the winter. It had no electricity, no heat, no plumbing, just damp beds and a bucket in the corner if we needed to pee in the night. My mother would take us over each night and lock us in until morning.

I was terrified every night all night for the six weeks of this ordeal. My mother had little patience for my fears. She was not an unkind woman but she pushed away whatever she couldn't fix as if it wasn't there. I had nightmares for years after we moved into a Portland suburb. I couldn't sleep if my parents weren't home. I couldn't sleep if the door to my room was closed and a light wasn't shining in from the hall. My mother had little patience for any of this either.

I know now that this was post-traumatic distress, but neither my mother nor I knew that then. The only remedy she knew was to tell me to "forget about it." I couldn't do that so I had to find another way to make myself feel better: food.

Experience #3

The new home near Portland meant a new school in the city. My early classroom experiences had been engaging and joyful. I had spent the first four years in a rural 3-room schoolhouse where classes were tiny (there were only five of us in my class: Mark, Linda, Buster, Kathy, and me). We got a lot of individual attention and we were free to wander around the room and find things to do when we had finished a particular lesson. Now I was in fifth grade in a regimented classroom in a city school. We were expected to sit still, be quiet, and fold our hands on top of the desk and wait while other children finished their work. We couldn't leave our desks without permission. We couldn't talk without permission. Already tortured at night, I was now tortured during the day.

3
ENTER SUGAR, ENTER ADDICTION

After a few weeks at that school, I discovered the Little Store, a corner market two long blocks from our house and I began spending all my allowance, plus coins I stole from my father's dresser, on candy. I went there after school any day I had money and on Saturdays too. The freedom of childhood in the 1950s helped make this possible. I could always go for a ride on my bike. It isn't long before I was eating the candy in school, sneaking it all day from a small paper bag in my desk, one of the convenient kind that had a large wooden lid that opens up away from the teacher.

By junior high, we had moved across town but there was still a candy store on my way to school. My mother had first taken me there herself. On that trip, she had given me a dime and told me to choose something for myself. I bought 10¢ worth of chunk milk chocolate. One bite and I was hooked. After that, each morning I left the house in plenty of time. My mother thought I was eager to get to school, but in reality, I needed the time to stop at the Sweet Shoppe. I was almost always the only customer at 8 am. Mrs. Elliott, the owner, never remarked about what I bought or how often I was there. Maybe she was glad to have the business. Maybe she understood what I needed.

I didn't know, of course, that I was medicating myself. I didn't know that I was establishing habits and brain patterns that would cost me dearly later on. I did know that I was doing something bad. I told no one about this. I hid the candy. It was not that I didn't want to share it, but I had to be sure I had enough. And I didn't want it taken away from me. I didn't want my behavior monitored. More habits and patterns got ingrained.

And I knew for sure that I felt better when I got as much candy as I wanted into my system. My fear, my restlessness, my boredom, all went away.

4
ADDICTION AND ANXIETY

As a child, I didn't know of course that what was happening to me was anxiety. I had a hard time sitting still, and my body was jittery a lot of the time. I didn't know that I had become hyper-vigilant. After the weeks of sleeping across the road in the Big House, I no longer trusted that my parents would be there for me and I didn't know how to talk to them about this. I was afraid of everything that I couldn't control so I tried to control everything. I went to bed at precise times. I checked the locks on the doors each night. I insisted that we have a fire escape plan. I learned the seven warning signs of cancer and continually checked myself for any sign.

My mother called my obsessive and compulsive behaviors "silly." In her mind, I should just get over it. I know she didn't want me to suffer, but she didn't have any way to understand what had happened to me, and I couldn't discuss my worries and fears with her. She clung to her own childhood belief that negative emotions came from too little to do, and she could always find more chores to give me.

For nearly a decade, candy was my best friend. It saved me from the rigidity and boredom of the classroom. It saved me from the seeming indifference of my parents. It saved me from some of the angst and loneliness of adolescence. In fact, candy saved my sanity. If I ate enough of it, the fear went away. I could concentrate on the sweetness and then when it was all gone, I could relax into the delicious feeling of being sated, of having had enough of what I wanted.

I had formed a tight bond with the salvation of sweets and I had learned how to take care of myself. When I discovered alcohol, that worked even better. And when I had to give alcohol up because it was killing me, my old pal sugar stepped right back onto center stage of my life.

5
SUGAR AND MY EARLY RECOVERY FROM ALCOHOLISM

In September 1989, I entered a treatment center in Lynchburg, Virginia. Wednesday that week I had finally told my doctor the extent of my drinking and she arranged for me to go into a 28-day treatment program. I checked in at 4 pm on Saturday, still drunk. At 8 pm, I went to my first 12-step meeting. I was offered a cup of coffee and a doughnut. I didn't accept either because I was pretty out of it, but the next night I felt better and I had both.

I went to two or three AA meetings a day the first year I was sober. Every meeting had coffee and sweets of some kind: doughnuts, cookies, cake, candy. The treatment center itself had had an endless supply of cookies and a chest freezer full of ice cream bars. We were encouraged to eat all we wanted. In fact, the counselors recommended that we keep candy around at home or in our purse and eat some if we felt a craving to drink, saying that we needed to substitute for the sugar we were used to consuming in the alcohol. (At an AA meeting recently, a list of helpful hints for surviving the holidays went around. Tip #9 was carry candy with you wherever you go.)

We were all adults, of course, and maybe their assumption was that we could eat sugar in moderation. But I don't think that was the case. I don't think any of them, from the nurses to the counselors, who were all in recovery themselves, thought about the fact that we had all proven already that we couldn't be moderate. Nor did they think about sugar as an addictive substance. Beside, putting on a few pounds was preferable to pounding down a few drinks in relapse.

That first year, my sugar of choice was midgie Tootsie Rolls. It's not very good candy and I'm not sure why that became my obsession, maybe because it was chewy, maybe because unwrapping each little piece (quiet wrappers that don't rustle) gave me something to do with my restlessness. I didn't eat them except in meetings but I'd go through a bag a meeting. With 730 meetings that first year, I must have eaten a truckload. I ate other sweet foods during the day sometimes. I don't much remember. It didn't worry me how much I ate. I wasn't drinking and that was all that mattered.

I'd also long known that staying really busy kept negative feelings at bay. My mom was right about that. So I tried hard to stay busy enough so that I could stay safe from alcohol. That busyness helped protect me from the agony of the slow decline of my 10-year relationship with my boyfriend, which I could see would not survive my sobriety. I thought that if I ate enough sweets and stayed busy enough, maybe I could stay sober and not mind that our life together was over. It seemed a winning formula.

I left that relationship after 10 months of sobriety. He'd gotten far more serious about one of his other women than he'd ever been about me, and I found a new teaching job 300 miles away. So I subtracted the jealousy and added loneliness. Of course I stayed connected to AA in my new town. More meetings, more cookies, more coffee. Evening meetings we went out for pie afterwards. Morning meetings we went out for pancakes. Nobody had a salad. Nobody had oatmeal. We ate sweets.

I often did well all day at work. The faculty dining hall served reasonable meals and I'd only occasionally buy a cookie or a piece of pie. But the evenings were tough. I'd get home about 4 and the AA meeting didn't start until 8. This was the cocktail hour, the drinking-as-transition time that I'd been doing for 20 years. So I started baking to fill the time. I got hooked on caramel brownies and would eat half a pan. I made cookies and consumed six or eight at a time—however many it took to get relief. The warm sweets gave me something to look forward to when I left my office.

Then in my third year of sobriety, my AA sponsor introduced me to Dove Bars on the drive back from an AA weekend rally. Dove Bars are an extraordinarily caloric ice cream bar. One bar and I was hooked. It became my drug of choice for nearly five years. I didn't care that I was putting on a few pounds, and then a few more, and then a few more. Although I wasn't staying healthy, I was staying sober and I was more at peace than I'd been in a long time.

6
SUGAR AND GETTING FAT

The weight gain didn't hit me in the beginning. I grew up thin. I was a bean pole kid, shooting up to 5'10" as I hit puberty and weighing about 110 pounds. My mother encouraged me to eat what I wanted because clearly it didn't show up as fat. In fact, there were no weight repercussions of my free-for-all with food until I hit 35, and even then it was fairly easy for me to take the weight off for quite a while, mostly thanks to chronic jealousy and anxiety from my unhealthy relationships with men who were no more emotionally available to me than my parents had been. More habits and patterns.

During my drinking decades, I looked like a normal eater. I ate three reasonable meals a day. I ate dessert when it was offered and if it was something I liked. I ate a candy bar or two; I'd have a donut or a scone. I actually preferred chips and dip or French fries, salty fat foods. This is not surprising because my sugar needs were being met by four bottles of wine a day. I'd overeat occasionally. Who doesn't? But the weight stayed off.

Some alcoholics stop eating as their disease progresses. I didn't. Drinking made me hungry, hungry for pizza, popcorn, burgers, French fries—again the fat and salt to balance out all that sugar. I kept a well-stocked refrigerator as well as a well-stocked liquor supply. The combination of food and alcohol was the best tranquilizer I could find. I wasn't ever tempted by anorexia and although I threw up every morning for years, I was not bulimic, just toxic. I needed to feel fed, to feel full in order to feel okay.

In 1994, at five years sober, the weight was coming on. I'd been gaining about half a pound a month since I got sober. Weight gain that slow is very easy to adjust to. Your clothes gradually get tighter. You look for a fuller cut of pants or a little looser top. Then, what the hell, you just buy an 18 or a 20 or a 22.

A couple of years later, I watched 200 go by on the scale, a number I swore I'd never see. But then it was easy to see 202 go by and 205 and 209. I'd think about getting on a diet, eating a little less, but I never took action. I didn't like the way I looked, but I liked the calm that so much sugar and fat gave me. I was starting to slow down but since I was trying to relax anyway—that's why we're eating what we do and as much as we do, isn't it?—that mild sluggishness seemed a good thing. I didn't have as much energy but I didn't have as much anxiety either. I wasn't working so hard. That all seemed good. Numb equals good.

FOOD FOR THOUGHT

1. How do you relate to the word *addicted*?
2. What experiences may have started you on the road to food addiction?
3. Why and how did you start self-medicating with food?
4. How did food serve you when you were younger?
5. How have sugar and other foods continued to serve you?
6. What is your history of weight gain?

NOTE: *The number of each question refers to the chapter with the same number. As you explore your own relationship to food addiction, these may be useful for journaling or talking about with your buddy or your small group.*

7
MY ADVENTURES IN DIETING, PART I

Dieting as a way of life was modeled in my home. My mother used all kinds of plans to lose weight. She ate a kind of chocolate candy called Ayds with a cup of instant coffee before dinner to control her appetite. She was an early Weight Watchers member who made her own ketchup from their recipe. She did Slimfast. One of my sisters was a thin stick like me; the other was heavy from the get-go. Both of them dieted with my mother when they were in their teens. I wasn't interested. I didn't need to lose weight yet, and I sure wasn't interested in restricting my sugar and fat intake.

In my late 20s, my boyfriend thought I would look better if I were thinner. He promised to buy me new clothes if I lost the weight. At 5'10" and 145, I was plenty thin enough already, but to please him, I dieted for about four months and lost about 15 pounds. I did it with a friend who also didn't need to lose weight. We counted calories and ate some of the then new frozen diet meals, and we took some aerobics classes and jazzercise at the university where we were graduate students. It was a kind of game.

My boyfriend was pleased, but I don't remember being any happier with my body. He did buy me the new clothes and I wore them briefly, but I couldn't sustain that weight. I couldn't eat that little for the long term. I was too hungry and too unhappy. We split up about six months later.

Single again, lonely, nervous, unhappy, I got thin again. I drank a lot, had a lot of sex, ate sporadically. When I fell in love, I started to gain weight back. Part of it was the reduction in anxiety, part of it was age. I was 35 and my youth was over and middle age was spreading itself all over me.

My new boyfriend and I ate and drank ourselves through the first year together. I added 15 pounds. I started jogging and then running. It helped me be able to continue to eat and drink. But the weight crept on: 2 pounds a year, 4 pounds a year, 6 pounds a year. I stopped eating big meals. Instead, I ate Lean Cuisine with my wine and sweets. I did this kind of half-assed dieting for another 5 years.

Then I got sober. I immediately lost some of the alcohol bloat but my candy and sweets consumption filled in the calorie gap with no trouble.

8
WHAT SUGAR ADDICTION LOOKED LIKE ON ME

It's a Saturday and I've been sober for eight years. I spent most of the morning at a drawing class. Then in my pastel-stained leggings and T-shirt, I went to my 12-Step home group at noon. Infused with the spirit and the support of my 12-step friends, I should be doing fine. But instead all I can feel is the empty weekend stretching out in front of me. No plans, no work that needs doing, no structure. On the way home, I stop at the store, going out of my way to find just what I need. In my grocery cart is a liter of diet soda, a package of sliced ham, a bag of caramels, and four boxes of milk chocolate Dove Bars.

When I get home, I eat lunch, a ham sandwich and some salad. Then I turn off the phone, get the novel I'm reading, and sit down in the big green velvet chair I call the sofa-for-one. I open the first Dove Bar, bite in, and relax into the sweetness. The dread of the long weekend ahead of me dissipates. I have a big supply of what I need to make it through. And in a very few minutes, I'm at the refrigerator, opening the freezer compartment and pulling out two more Dove Bars. I return to the green chair and my book.

Half an hour goes by. If you'd walked in on me, you'd have assumed I was absorbed in reading. But my mind is only half attending to the story. The other half is standing in front of the refrigerator, calculating how many of the Dove Bars I can eat and not feel sick. Going into the afternoon, I had promised myself that I would only eat two bars. At the same time, I knew this was a joke, for I had bought 4 packages of Dove Bars, 16 in all, and I know from years and years of experience, first with sugar and then with alcohol and then with sugar again, that what I have I will consume. I get up and get a fourth Dove Bar, finishing the first package. I go back to my book.

Although I'll eat sugar indiscriminately—cookies that aren't my favorite, an ice cream or pie that I don't really like—I don't consider that part of my addiction. That's just what's offered. Instead, my addiction normally has a single focus, a current object of my obsession. For three years, that obsession has been with Dove Bars.

It isn't until I take the last Dove Bar out of the second package that it registers that I have now eaten eight of them. This makes me uneasy. I tally up in my mind the fat grams and calories, and it frightens me. I think vaguely of my heart and my arteries. But I am feeling very full and sleepy and so about 4 pm, I lie down and sleep a couple of hours. When I wake up, I don't feel very good. I fix some soup and crackers and cheese, something salty to offset all the sweets. I watch some TV. But my mind is really focused on the other two packages of ice cream bars in the freezer.

About 8:30 the TV loses all interest and I find myself pacing the kitchen floor. I'm not the least bit hungry, I'd eaten my supper with very little appetite, but I cannot stop thinking about the Dove Bars. It's as if they are calling my name. I eat one more.

The nap earlier that afternoon has given me a second wind so I watch TV until late. I avoid the kitchen. I get ready for bed. Then I remember how good the Dove Bars taste with freshly brushed teeth. I get into bed with my book but I can't stop thinking about the seven that remain. Even though it is after midnight, in the next 20 minutes, I eat three more.

When I get up on Sunday morning, I swear off. I have some coffee and make some eggs and toast. I go for a long walk in the park. I come back and do the laundry and clean house. I feel okay. I sweep the terrace and the garage. I balance my checkbook. I grocery shop at my usual market, the one that only carries dark chocolate Dove Bars. I don't like dark chocolate. I buy healthy food. I get home about 4 pm and put away the groceries and arrange the flowers I've bought. The house looks nice.

I sit down with my book in the green chair but all I can think about is that fourth package of Dove Bars in the fridge. I last about 10 minutes and then I have suddenly eaten all four and I am in my car on the way to the other supermarket. I feel guilty and ashamed and worried about the impact of all of this fat on my health and yet I cannot stop. I buy two more packages. There needs to be enough, there needs to be extra.

When I'm in relapse

Couldn't do it
Couldn't stay away
From the frozen
Where my favorites
Were on sale
It wasn't spontaneous
That decision
I'd itched towards it all afternoon
The nudge
The niggle
Picking up steam after lunch
I needed to go anyway
Prescriptions to pick up
Cat food
Printer paper
But I didn't need ice cream
But, well, yes, I did
And the relief comes
So quickly
The decision made
So easily
The cart full
So smoothly
And the remorse
Still hours away

9
MY ADVENTURES IN DIETING, PART II

Although I did stop eating Dove Bars, I really just switched obsessions: Snickers bars, then Snickers ice cream bars, a particular kind of cake, some toffee-laden cookies. There's no end of sugar to obsess about.

A year later, I resolved to get off sugar. It wasn't that I had suddenly realized I was fat and needed to lose some weight. I was becoming worried—seriously worried—about my health. I didn't have to be a mathematician to figure out I was consuming large quantities of animal fat (ice cream is, after all, animal fat). I'd gone on medications for high cholesterol and high blood pressure. I could pretend it was genetic, but I knew that consuming a half-dozen candy bars or three gigantic cookies or a gallon of ice cream every afternoon was implicated as well.

I'd given up alcohol because I could see that it was killing me. Now I didn't want suicide by caramel swirl. So I committed to six months of abstinence from desserts. That included morning desserts like pancakes and scones and muffins. I didn't give up incidental sugar, the sugar that might occur in a spaghetti sauce or in a little jam on my toast, but I gave up anything that could become a binge food.

I got through Thanksgiving and my birthday and Christmas and a writing retreat that had catered sweets three times a day. It became easier to say no as the time went on. I just didn't eat that stuff. I lost some weight, and I felt better. In addition, my emotional and spiritual life seemed much more on track, an unexpected bonus.

But then the six months were up and I was faced with myself again. And I found myself bingeing and swearing off and feeling crappy and lost again. Part desire, part habit, part wish to be irresponsible and relax my now chronic hyper-vigilance, using sugar to soothe my feelings was so ingrained that I couldn't stop.

About this time, I found a food plan guaranteed to keep me off sugar forever. It was called the *5-Day Miracle Diet* and in it, nutritionist Adele Puhn walks the reader through the miserable five days it takes to get off sugar. She recommends a very healthy diet of whole foods and grains and nothing fried; then after a month you can have sugar in moderation. Because, according to Puhn, it's too hard to abstain completely from sweets (after all, there are celebrations and special occasions where desserts are an important part of life), she recommended that after a month or two, I'd be able to have a small piece of whatever I wanted once or twice a week. Wow! Just the license I was hoping for.

    I abstained from all sugar for four months, lost nearly 40 pounds, and then introduced Puhn's once-a-week idea. I'd carefully wait for Saturday, the end of my week, and then have that piece of pie or piece of cake or bowl of ice cream. But as the weeks went by, I would get invited out on a Tuesday for a friend's birthday or anniversary or promotion or baby shower or wedding or just because, and I'd have dessert. And now Saturday loomed bleak and empty and so I decided that twice a week would be okay, And that lasted maybe another month and then I was finding all kinds of ways to play with Puhn's rule.

    Instead of being my salvation, Puhn's book was the catalyst for my foray into yo-yo dieting. I don't fault her or her book. Nobody, including Puhn, made me do it. However, she held out the tantalizing promise of occasional sugar consumption, the promise that moderation around sugar is possible. Moderation is always possible—unless you're an addict. The truth is that we—I—don't want moderation. I don't want to have a drink once in a while. I want to drink all I want whenever I want. I don't want one caramel. I want the package. I want it until I don't want it.

    After my failure with Puhn's program, I gave up and I just ate whatever I wanted. It was such a relief to stop struggling.

FOOD FOR THOUGHT

7 When and how did you get into dieting?

8 What experience from your past or present comes to mind that can represent your experience with sugar addiction?

9 Is there a time when you knew you couldn't eat sugar or other foods in moderation and you just gave up struggling to be normal?

We don't really want to be free from desire or to admit that clinging to the pleasures of the senses—the taste of delicious food; the sound of music, gossip, or a joke; the touch of a sexual embrace—ends unavoidably in disappointment and suffering.

—Bhante Gunaratana

10
GIVING UP SUGAR AGAIN AND AGAIN

In 2010, on Valentine's Day, I tried again. Again, I gave up desserts. I made my decision public in my blog (www.sobertruths.blogspot.com) as I struggled for a few weeks. I ate a lot of other kinds of foods, but eventually the strong physiological need for sugar passed. And I went nearly three years without any. Oh, I had substitutes: toast with all fruit jam, low sugar granola bars, snack bars made with dates, dried fruit, but none of it was yummy enough to be worth a binge.

I initially lost about 20 pounds when I got off sugar. The weight left slowly (I didn't have a scale). Then, after a few months, I could feel it coming back on. Why? Because I was substituting all kinds of other foods to get sated: burgers and fries, grilled cheese sandwiches, chips and dip. I was still bingeing, still overeating, just not sugar. It became sadly and painfully clear to me that it wasn't just sweets I was addicted to. I was also addicted to many kinds of food because of the way they made me feel.

In 2013, my friend Sue introduced me to the documentaries *Forks over Knives* and *Fat, Sick, and Nearly Dead*. Then an old 12-Step friend contacted me to say she was doing nutrition work. She had healed herself from Lyme's disease and was reaching out to others who wanted to improve their health through better eating. Because she had been a long time in recovery from alcohol and because she said she saw herself as a food addict, I hired her to help me. I knew I was eating the wrong foods and I needed support to figure that out. I got off wheat and dairy, commonly believed to be the big problem for most folks. I lost about 30 pounds and felt great, so great that I started drafting this book. I thought I was cured.

However, while I was eating a lot better, I was still resistant to any conversation about how much I ate or how often I ate. I wanted it to be simple: change what I eat and lose weight and then start over with moderation. And I didn't ever want to be hungry. I also had nowhere to go with my emotional relationship with food. And it became clear that my coach really wasn't a food addict, as I understand it or—

perhaps more accurately—as I live it. She was an occasional overeater of French fries who had never been fat.

About six months into this last failed attempt, I went to Florida to teach a couple of writing workshops to recovering women. The friend I stayed with has a husband who's a recovering alcoholic with many years of sobriety and a well-grooved candy habit. She herself doesn't suffer with sugar, and of course, she knows we can't change someone else so there was a lot of candy around their house. I thought I was strong enough to handle the exposure. But canisters of candy on the kitchen counter, candy at our workshops for the lunch boxes, cookies in the box lunches. I didn't have the will power or the conviction, so I told myself I would get back on my plan when I got home. And for a few weeks, I did. And then I set foot on an even slipperier slope and I was right back in it. I came back home and slowly regained the 30 pounds plus 15 more. I still hadn't grasped the fact that the food itself is not the issue.

For the last few weeks, I've been back on sugar, in true candy girl fashion. I have not been in denial but I have been in defiance, so I haven't written about it, because I knew that once I did, once I admitted it to someone other than myself, I would be on the way to abstinence again and I don't want to be abstinent from sugar. Cunning, baffling, and powerful, as we say in 12-Step meetings. The cunning, baffling, and powerful link between the need and the hell, yes, why not? and the consequences be damned. PS. In true addict fashion, I had to make sure I had eaten all my sugar stash before I wrote this entry.

—From my journal

11
DEALING WITH MY OWN ENTRENCHED RESISTANCE

A first step for me was fully admitting my resistance. I had been beaten up, whipped by alcohol and had come to a place where I could admit my powerlessness over it and give it up. Now I was becoming convinced that I was a sugar addict, that I just can't eat the stuff. As I've said, I'd been off recreational sugars for extended times—three years at one point—and while I relapsed, it was no longer because I was fooling myself into believing I was cured. I would just lapse into insanity either briefly or for a fairly long period of time and then get back in the abstinence saddle. I even became okay accepting responsibility for all the extra weight I was carrying from the sugar.

But unequivocally, categorically, I didn't want to be a food addict. I didn't want one more problem, one more program, one more burden. I didn't want to have to be hyper-vigilant about what I eat, how much I eat, and when I eat it. I didn't want another addiction, plain and simple. But of course, that's not how it works. That's not where my choices lie.

An important review in the *Journal of Nutrition* in 2013 presented this statement:[1] "Overweight or obese individuals probably do meet the clinical criterion for food addiction if they experience a persistent desire to quit or repeated unsuccessful attempts to quit; have given up or reduced important social, occupational, or recreational activities; or continue to use despite the knowledge of adverse consequences." This describes me to a T: repeated unsuccessful attempts and continued use despite the knowledge of the health and well-being consequences. My wanting it to not be so doesn't matter. I have this addiction too.

---

[1] http://jn.nutrition.org/content/139/3/620.short

12
WHAT I STILL NEEDED TO FIGURE OUT

As I passed 290 on the scale and had to face that I knew exactly how I'd gotten there, I despaired that there was any kind of solution. I wrote a second draft of this book talking about just that: how no diet works, how the struggle with food is inevitable. It was realistic and well written, but something in me couldn't move forward with a book of such resignation and limited hope. So I set it aside and kept eating. Then a friend sent me a link to the introductory videos of Bright Line Eating, an online program for food addicts, and the missing pieces began to fall into place. I got hopeful and I started to lose both weight and my despair.

Here are some of the things I was figuring out:
- Accepting and embracing that I was addicted to some foods as self-medication was essential.
- No diet plan alone could free me from my unhealthy relationship with sugar and flour and other trigger foods. Food is not the problem.
- Dieting is not abstinence, but abstinence for a food addict can be a whole lot simpler than I thought.
- Snacks aren't good for me; trying to lose a lot of weight and never be hungry is unrealistic.
- I had to change how I ate, not just what I ate.
- How I live my life is key to recovery, not just how I eat.

FOOD FOR THOUGHT

10 Is there a time when you thought you were cured of sugar/food addiction?

11 What resistance must you face to step fully into recovery?

12 What mistaken beliefs or misunderstandings have kept you hooked on food?

When relapse stops working

I've been having a fling with an old lover
We said goodbye some years ago
He promised not to come around
And I promised not to let him
But then on the brink
Of sorting it all out
For once, for good
I saw him in the grocery store
He looked great
And that small voice
Inside me
You know the one
So cunning, so powerful
Shouted out
Come on over!
Bring your friends!
And just like that
They were riding in the cart
Going through check-out
Filling up the passenger seat
Taking up room in the freezer
We've had a good time
He's always a good time
But it's not working out
As well as I hoped
Each time I go to the store
He's waiting for me
And one little evening
Has turned into a thing between us
An affair
And he wants to move in for good
But I can't do it
I just can't do it anymore
And live with myself

CANDY GIRL

IS SUGAR ADDICTION REAL?

13
A LITTLE ABOUT RESEARCH ON SUGAR AND ADDICTION

After two decades of struggle, I acknowledged more than 27 years ago that I was addicted to alcohol. I found my way to treatment and to the 12 Steps as a philosophy for living. I seldom feel the desire for a drink and almost never have a compulsive urge to have one. I am so grateful for that.

It also makes sense to me that I am a sugar addict. I have medicated with different forms of sugar for most of my conscious life. I have probably eaten more sweets than 10,000 normal people at Halloween. If you've read this far, you've seen how I've used and overused it.

In addition, research has shown that sugar seems to have a comparable effect on the brain to alcohol and heroin. Sugar consumption lights up the reward center of the brain, releasing dopamine, a feel-good brain chemical in a multi-step process just like alcohol and drugs do. And like alcohol and drugs, we have to keep upping the quantity we ingest to keep getting the same good feeling. So the one Dove Bar that was so delicious, so soothing, so numbing became, over five years, four boxes a day.

Many years ago, a friend told me of a man she knew at her AA meetings in southern Oregon. The man had been successfully sober for over 30 years but he could not stop using sugar. Not after he was diagnosed with diabetes, not after a leg was amputated, not after he started to go blind. He died during surgery for the second leg amputation. I have not forgotten that story.

14
A BIT MORE ABOUT RESEARCH

Other research has shown that some of us process refined carbohydrates like sugar and flour inappropriately with a negative impact on the pancreas organ, leading us towards insulin resistance and possible diabetes. It is also probably not a coincidence that populations with high levels of diabetes also have high levels of alcoholism since both conditions involve the body's processing of sugars.

In one research study, a dozen obese men consumed milkshakes on two different occasions. The milkshakes made with high-fructose corn syrup not only raised their blood sugar levels more quickly than the low-glycemic milkshakes did, but four hours later, their blood sugar levels had plummeted into the hypoglycemic (low blood sugar) range, the subjects reported more hunger, and brain scans showed greater activation in those parts of their brains that regulate cravings, reward, and addictive behaviors. The most telling piece of information? Every subject showed the same response.

When hypoglycemia hits us, we tend to seek out foods that will raise it again quickly, and more sugar is a fast way to do it. I also suspect that those of us with a lot of sugar experience have shortened that four-hour window to next to nothing by developing higher levels of tolerance. Such cravings are in part physiological; there's a strong signal from our bodies that they need something. The cravings are real—they are a physical discomfort; the body does need fixing. We don't call it a *fix* for no reason.

15
HOW MUCH PROOF DO WE NEED THAT WE SUFFER?

I find such research convincing because it explains my behaviors. The medical profession is slow to change and these studies are few and small, so the establishment isn't jumping on the sugar addiction band wagon. But that doesn't matter to me.

I am convinced that I can't eat sugar and flour in moderation. I can't leave it alone once I start. I've tried and tried and tried, and I can't. I just can't no matter how much I want to.

We food addicts know that we struggle. We know that we keep swearing off and relapsing, that we eat compulsively and obsessively whatever our trigger foods are. And we know that will power and discipline are not enough even though our culture wants us to believe that they are. Scientific proof that this is addiction is not necessary for me to define my dilemma.

And that dilemma is a rather simple one. Eat sugar and flour and suffer or don't eat them and live with peace and contentment.

All the research has shown that when people binge on carbs and sugar, and then restrict, the body creates an endogenous opioid. It is released in the body much like the chemicals released when people are doing other narcotics. The PET and CAT scans of food addicts look almost identical to that of alcoholics and drug addicts, showing that sugar creates a physical addiction. In addition, sugar addicts carry the same D2 dopamine receptor, the gene that identifies addiction, as alcoholics and addicts. In those ways, biochemically, food addiction is just like addiction to drugs and alcohol.

— Phil Werdell, co-founder of ACORN
Food Dependency Recovery Services

FOOD FOR THOUGHT

13 How have you had to keep upping your consumption of your trigger foods?

14 How do you use food to soothe your cravings?

15 Are you waiting for scientific proof before you can accept that sugar is an addiction?

16
ADDICTION MAKES US IRRATIONAL

We addicts face another problem. Our addictive behaviors are not rational. No one in her right mind eats herself to the point of pain night after night. No one figures out the number of grams of fat and sugar in what she's eating, is horrified, and consumes another package.

Addiction isn't something you can talk your way out of. It doesn't work to try to be rational about something that is not rational. I can't reason my way out of this rut. It's too comfortable, too familiar. When I'm in the terrible combination of emotional pain and physical craving, the soothing becomes paramount and nothing else matters.

In an interesting film called *What the Bleep*, an animated section demonstrates how neural pathways in our brains get laid down as we create habits. These pathways become ruts of a sort, so that when we encounter the same situation, we just follow along that pathway. This is really helpful for things like driving, where we need to be able to count on mental and physical memory to help us with the complex behaviors it takes to safely drive a car.

It's not so helpful when we create ruts of response to cravings. But the good news of the film was describing the exciting and life-saving ability of our brains and nervous systems to let disused pathways—or habits—die off and new neural pathways be created. This means that every time I step back into sugar, I reactivate the old pathways, but every time I do a new healthier habit, I can reinforce a new pathway. This creates a place of choice for me, for all of us.

On the *Forks over Knives* website, Dr. Doug Lisle posted an interesting article about cravings, noting the power of self-destructive cravings:

Cravings direct us to close the distance between ourselves and the target stimulus, essentially pulling our behavior toward satisfying the craving. That's how it's supposed to work. Unfortunately, cravings don't know the difference between healthy, natural targets and self-destructive ones... Your cravings are derived from images for pleasurable things. They are just the minions of your imagination. If the imagined targets involve artificially intense pleasure, those cravings can lead us to unhealthy decisions and lifestyles. For example, soda and ice cream provide us with a hyper-normal amount of pleasure and can trigger destructive cravings.

He's talking about me.

17
ARE YOU A SUGAR OR FOOD ADDICT?

This is a question each of us has to answer for ourselves. Maybe you just like to eat. We almost all do. We're wired that way as humans. But some of us are also wired to eat excessively, to eat compulsively. And that becomes a problem, especially in a culture with abundant food available on practically every street corner. In fact, it is far easier to be a food addict in a developed country than it is to be an alcoholic or a drug addict. Our poisons—sugar and flour foods made with fat—are plentiful and cheap. And they're not only legal but encouraged.

Here are some questions that may help:
1. Do you swear off sugar and flour products from time to time only to relapse in a few days, months, or years?
2. Do you hide what you are eating from other people?
3. Do you eat in secret and perhaps prefer it that way?
4. Do you bury the evidence (stuff wrappers into the bottom of a trash can, for example) so no one will know?
5. Do you feel guilty or ashamed of what and how much you eat?
6. Do you obsess about particular foods, perhaps going out of your way to buy just the right thing?
7. Do you feel a sense of emotional relief when you have plenty of those foods on hand?
8. Do you eat foods you say you are not going to eat?
9. With certain foods, are you unable to stop at one serving?
10. Do you suffer because of how and how much you eat?

This is not a scientific survey. This is a list of things I do as a food addict. At a recent women's retreat where I shared about my sugar addiction, a thin woman in her early 50s approached me and asked if I thought she might be a sugar addict. She didn't have a weight problem and wanted to know if that was proof enough that she wasn't addicted. I asked her the questions above. Her answer to every one was a yes.

How many of your answers are yes?

18
THE HARD WORK OF THE ACTIVE ADDICT

It takes a lot to be an active addict. We have to lie, sneak, hide our substance, make sure we have enough for all circumstances. We have to pretend we're all right when we aren't. And over the years of our active addiction, we build up a life that supports that addiction. We put all the pieces in place so we can go on eating (or drinking, gambling, drugging) in our addictive way.

We gather around us friends who eat the way we do. We encourage others to eat dessert too so we have an excuse for one. Then we order a second to go for "later" or "for a friend or spouse" knowing all the time we're going to eat it in the car. We find a spouse who turns a blind eye to our addictive behaviors or who shares them. We spend more and more time alone because it's just easier. Or we live alone. That's the easiest of all.

At work, we bring treats and encourage others to do so. We celebrate everybody's birthday, every holiday, every Friday with treats. We become the party planners so we can be sure there will be plenty for us. We're the one with the candy dish on our desk and the extra bags in the bottom drawer. We become experienced bakers, candy makers, amateur chefs. We can be counted on to bring the best desserts and treats. That becomes our specialty.

All of this contributes to a life that supports food addiction. Diets ask us to stop doing our addiction. To stop overeating, bingeing, purging. But they don't help us change the life that we've so carefully constructed to support that addiction.

To keep up an active addiction, we have to live our lives in a certain way. For example, addiction loves chaos. An erratic schedule is a big part of that: no regular meal times or bed times. We work too little or work too much. We have a love/hate relationship with responsibility. We rail against it, hating the obligation. Yet we want to be successful in the world, in our families. We want to be treated like adults.

True recovery asks us to take responsibility for our choices, all our choices, and make them in service to our own well-being. And that may well involve some hard decisions.

FOOD FOR THOUGHT

16 Which of your behaviors with food seem irrational to you?

17 What do your answers to the quiz tell you?

18 What hard decisions might come your way as you contemplate recovery?

BREAKING FREE

19
WHY I THINK MOST DIETS DON'T WORK

Food addiction appears to be about food. But it is not. This is the primary reason that diets don't work. Food is not the problem.

If we set aside all the ludicrous and extreme diets (two weeks of cabbage soup or eating only spinach and grapefruit, for example), if we eliminate the drugs, pills, and patches to suppress appetite (often forms of amphetamine), we're looking at a handful of programs with a very similar success rate. Weight Watchers, Jenny Craig, LA Weight Loss, Atkins. Research shows that the number of people who lose all the weight they want in each of these programs hovers around 10% of those who sign up. The number who keep that weight off is often much lower. This same success rate is true of Overeaters Anonymous and other 12-Step programs for addicts as well.

Most of the programs that charge for their plan or foods aren't really interested in finding out why. Who can blame them? These are for-profit businesses, selling the promise of weight loss, not the reality. If the programs really worked, they'd be out of business. But even researchers are baffled by how people lose weight—some or a lot—and then gain it back. They've looked for all kinds of physiological reasons why the body won't let itself stay thinner. But I don't believe the answer lies in the body. Here are my thoughts.

Reason #1: Diets concentrate on what's measurable: calories consumed and expended, the chemical interaction of certain foods on each other (food combining), limiting quantities, measuring hormones in the blood. How many grams of fat, how many of protein. How big portions should be (a thumb of this, a fist of that, the palm of your hand or a deck of cards of yet another food). **Our real problem is not measurable.**

Reason #2: Diets are about information, much of it scientific. They teach and preach nutrition, often information that contradicts itself. We should eat more vegetables, follow a pyramid of foods. We should cut out eggs because they have fat and cholesterol. We should eat more eggs because they are an excellent source of protein and vitamins. Eat lettuce but only certain kinds. Eat more protein but less meat. Eat only certain sources of fat. But most food addicts are not ignorant about nutrition. **A lack of information is not our problem.**

Reason #3: Diets focus on the wrong thing. They focus on what we eat and how much we eat. They propose quantities and combinations. Sometimes these are sound ideas, sometimes not. **But for a food addict, why we eat is our problem.**

The Big Book of Alcoholics Anonymous has a wonderful comment on the futility of some of our efforts in dealing with addiction: "We thought we would find an easier, softer way. But we could not." Dieting for me was the easier, softer way. Change what I eat and I'd be cured. It turned out that that was a lie.

20
THE MOST IMPORTANT REASON DIETS DON'T WORK

Diets and food plans and fasting and pills and patches don't work because they don't attend to the most serious problem we addicts face: the life we are living.

There's a long-standing joke in recovery programs: Give an addict a rut and he'll furnish it. Carpeting, big-screen TV, recliner, you name it. We get stuck in our ways no matter how miserable they are. As active addicts, we have established, created, and maintained lives, ruts, and habits that support our addictive behavior. We have relationships, jobs, finances, hobbies, stresses, families, lives that keep the need for the soothing going.

Giving up the food or alcohol or gambling is just a start. It's the life that has to change. The life that supports addiction has to shift into a life that supports recovery. And to have a new life, we have to give up, partly, mostly, or entirely, the life we have. This is a terrifying thought for most of us.

21
WHAT IT TAKES TO BREAK FREE

Some people are able to see addiction coming at them before it gets ugly, but most of us don't have a clue. I didn't. Addiction very often starts in childhood. It did for me. I'm not saying that small children are drinking alcohol or shooting up heroin or sneaking into high-stakes poker games. I'm saying they're experiencing trauma, big or small. They're experiencing insecurities beyond the norm, fears and sensitivities that incline them to seek relief to survive. Some of this may be in their temperament; they are born with certain tendencies, certain responses. But much of this is provoked by their environment—family, school, city or town, the culture.

Food, very often sweets, are the only drug readily available to most of us as kids, and so we begin to self-medicate. We establish the neural pathway, the habit, of taking care of ourselves in the easiest way possible. This is usually unconscious. Even if we sense that this isn't right, like I did (I learned to sneak and hide my candy very early on), we don't know what else to do and so we deepen the mental groove. All this occurs for emotional survival.

Over the years, a number of possible solutions presented themselves to me to deal with my weight gain. A friend would recommend a book. I would hear about an acquaintance's success with a coach or food plan. I would go to a few 12-Step meetings on food. But I didn't hear what I needed. Not yet. I wasn't ready. I was too terrified to give up the familiar. The salvation I'd been using still worked—sort of. I still got numb. But its side effects were increasingly troublesome—more and more excess weight, more serious health problems, discrimination as an obese person in a thin-oriented society. Yet I couldn't imagine life without that relief.

And that's the crux of the matter. To step into real recovery, the first essential is imagination. We have to be able to imagine a life without sweets, without bingeing, without overeating, without that relief. We have to be able to imagine building a life that needs less relief and one in which we can find alternate ways to get that relief when we do need it.

We don't have to be able to imagine ourselves thin, but we must be able to imagine ourselves feeling okay no matter what happens and without food. We have to be able to imagine ourselves able to respond in different ways to what happens. We have to learn to imagine ourselves free.

FOOD FOR THOUGHT

19 Why do you think diets haven't worked for you in the past?

20 What comes up for you when you think about having to change your life in order to recover from sugar and food addiction?

21 How has a lack of imagination kept you imprisoned in your addiction?

22
SAYING IT AND ACCEPTING IT ARE NOT THE SAME THING

As I said earlier, *addiction* and *being addicted* are terms that many people use rather loosely. They're often used to describe things that are pleasurable and something we want again, like a pedicure or a TV show. But for the millions of us who suffer from addiction, from the compulsion and obsession, from the physical and emotional consequences, these words are serious business. And it's because of that seriousness that I too used the word loosely for a long time. My doing so wasn't meant to be cute or clever. It was an attempt to deny the seriousness of what was happening to me.

I didn't want to see that the tootsie rolls and the cake and the cookies I ate after work in early sobriety were another addiction, or really, part of the same addiction. I didn't want to see that my Dove Bar obsession was an obsession although it was playing out that way right in front of me. I could admit that I had a problem with sugar. I had trouble staying away from it. I had difficulties with moderation. I compared it to buying five books at the bookstore instead of one or checking out three videos instead of one. I just like to have a lot of choice. But I did not want it to be an addiction. Because I know what happens to addicts. They endure a living hell or die, or they get abstinent.

I'd done the living hell with alcohol; I'd gotten abstinent. I knew it was possible.

But I didn't want to give up sugar. Even with undeniable proof that I couldn't leave it alone, that I couldn't have a piece of something and let that be it, I still didn't want to be addicted to sugar. "Not that, not that too!" I said over and over, both to myself and anyone who would listen.

People in alcohol recovery don't talk about sugar. We pretend it's an outside issue. It's not about alcohol. But of course it's related, more directly than drugs or gambling or sex. The Overeaters Anonymous meetings I went to years ago didn't talk about sugar either. At the time, I was glad. I interpreted that to mean that it wasn't the real problem.

Overeating was. That's what OA is about: Overeaters Anonymous. But by my definition, I wasn't a compulsive eater. There were lots of foods that I didn't eat compulsively. Of course my definition was skewed in the direction I wanted it to be.

Sometime late in 2013, I admitted that I was a sugar addict. At that point, I didn't know what the solution was. My previous efforts had failed. Weight Watchers didn't work. OA didn't work. Having a nutrition coach didn't work. Cutting out desserts didn't work. And I didn't personally know anyone else who struggled in the way I did. I still hadn't fully accepted it. I'd admitted it but not accepted it. Accepting meant doing something and I couldn't see what that would be.

23
IT TAKES WHAT IT TAKES TO BE WILLING

All 12-Step programs are full of slogans. "One day at a time." "Keep it simple." "It takes what it takes." This last refers to all the misery that most of us have to go through to accept the reality of addiction and seek recovery.

I can accept now that I had to be stuck for a long time. It was my path. Some people can surrender and get into recovery more quickly and they suffer less. Some of us stay stubborn and resistant for a longer time. We have to be ready.

When I went to Overeaters Anonymous a decade ago, I wasn't ready for it to work for me. I wasn't willing to get involved in the arm of that program that deals with sugar and flour. In fact, I didn't understand until recently that flour is a serious issue for me. I'd gone gluten-free for a while with no discernible change in my health or my weight. I didn't know that it was all pulverized grains that are problematic for me.

When I worked with a nutrition coach two years ago, I wasn't ready. I didn't want to have to be hungry to lose weight. I didn't want to stick to three meals a day. I didn't want portion control. I still wanted to eat all I wanted and have no consequences. I wasn't yet ready.

24
WE AREN'T READY UNTIL WE'RE READY

I don't know what makes us ready to shift, to change, to surrender. In my case, both with alcohol and with food, it was an encounter. In the first instance, my doctor asked me a direct question about alcohol consumption, something she had not asked before. I was ready and willing to tell her the truth, and that honesty led me into a treatment center and long-term sobriety.

In the second instance, it was a friend sending me a video about Bright Line Eating, where a charismatic recovering drug, sugar, and food addict named Susan Peirce Thompson described her problem, and her problem was my problem.

I almost didn't sign up for Susan's program. It was expensive and I was so resigned to failure. But a good friend encouraged me. "What if this is the answer?" she said. "What if this is the best money you ever spend?"

I'm really glad I listened. I was sick and tired of being sick and tired of overeating and struggling with food. I was finally ready to surrender and change.

FOOD FOR THOUGHT

22 What have you been saying to yourself and others about your struggle that denies its seriousness?

23 How ready are you to take recovery from food and sugar addiction seriously? Are you ready for freedom?

24 If you're not ready for recovery, how much more misery will it take?

THE OBSTACLES TO OVERCOME

25
CREATING AN ENVIRONMENT FOR CHANGE

One of the more provocative ideas in Robert Lustig's *Fat Chance: Beating the Odds against Sugar, Processed Food, Obesity, and Disease* is that behavior modification doesn't work all that well. We can change our behaviors: we can eat less, put the fork down between bites, sip water every other mouthful, knit or crochet in front of the TV, go for a long walk every day. But those behaviors alone aren't enough to make major changes in our health or our weight.

The key, he believes, is in changing our environment. Easy enough to do, you may say. I'll just clean out my cupboards of all the sugar and flour. And that's a good start. But it's only a start.

The 12-Step programs have known this principle for a long time. One of the first lectures I was sober enough to pay attention to in the treatment center was called "Change your playgrounds, change your playmates." If you want to stay sober, you don't go to bars or keggers or cocktail parties. You don't hang out with the same people you drank with, because they're probably going to go on drinking or hanging out at poker games or going by Sees Candy for that free sample every 20 minutes when they're at the mall.

But I know from my own experience that changing our environment often means a lot more than that. It can mean getting out of a dysfunctional or abusive relationship. I had to. It can mean changing careers. I did that too. It can mean moving to a new location where you've never been drunk. That helped me. And now I'm seeing that there's more.

First, there are the habits that don't serve me very well. Here are some of the habits I've had to let go of:

- Eating when I'm not hungry
- Bingeing on special foods
- Eating while I watch TV
- Eating whenever I feel like it
- Eating whatever I want

- Pretending I'm eating in a moderate and healthy way when I'm not
- Eating in secret
- Eating to put myself into a food coma so I can nap

Then there are the things I've had to add. As a fiercely independent and self-reliant person, I knew I'd have to get out more, call friends on the phone, share myself and my vulnerabilities in meetings and groups. None of that seemed the least bit easy. But if we're going to create an environment that supports recovery, we have to involve others in our life. We have to share any feelings that, left unspoken, may trigger a relapse.

26
CHANGING MY ENVIRONMENT HELPED ME LET GO OF FOOD AS A CRUTCH

A year ago, I got swept up in the decluttering mania that Marie Kondo's book, *The Life-Changing Magic of Tidying Up*, brought into the media spotlight. I'd sorted and reduced and purged my stuff over and over, but here was a woman with a method that offered longer-lasting results. You keep only what brings you joy and you discard the rest. And you only bring into your environment things that bring you joy.

I followed her ideas. It was a great game to play. And my apartment felt better and better, lighter and lighter. I went through the process twice, once to get rid of stuff and the second time to assign a place to everything so that I could get in the habit of putting things away after I used them. It was an interesting exercise in discipline and I had no idea it would lead me to weight loss and recovery from food addiction.

Looking back now, I can see how letting go of a lot of excess stuff and then following the discipline of caring for the stuff I had by treating it better and putting it away got me ready to recover. Lightening up my environment helped me be ready and willing to lighten up my body. Changing my habits with my stuff helped me be ready and willing to change my habits with eating.

The way into successful recovery often appears harder than continuing with our compulsive eating. Letting go of long-standing habits is no piece of cake (pun intended). There can be many obstacles in the path to freedom. Here are some I've encountered.

- Self-sabotage
- Sabotage from family and friends
- Unhelpful professionals
- Cultural sabotage
- Environmental sabotage

FOOD FOR THOUGHT

25-26 What changes to your environment could you make that might support your way into recovery from food addiction?

27
SELF-SABOTAGE: ENTITLEMENTS

We often think of entitlement as something other people have. *My son thinks he's entitled to live here for free as long as he wants. Those people think they're entitled to a handout from the government.* We seldom think about our own sense of entitlement or apply it to our beliefs about food.

I'd never stopped to think about my own entitlements until I went to a workshop a year ago. We were talking about our entitlements around money: *I make it and I can spend it anyway I want to. I work hard and it's mine.* And as I sat there, I began to think about the entitlement that is running my compulsive eating, an entitlement that lies below my conscious choices: *I should be able to eat anything I want whenever I want.* When I'm gripped by that entitlement, I am gripped by my addiction to eat.

The key words here are "should be able to." Any time we're in the land of *should*, we're not in reality. There's a world of difference between *I should eat less* and *I am eating less*. One is wishful thinking, the other is reality backed by action.

28
SELF-SABOTAGE: JUSTIFICATIONS

We can be equally sabotaged by our *unexamined justifications*. These seem like the truth and sometimes a part of them is true, but only a part. More importantly, because we want to believe them, we don't stop to think about them as self-sabotage.

- *It's my birthday so I can have cake. Everybody gets cake on their birthday.*
- *I worked hard. I deserve a treat. Everyone needs a treat now and then.*
- *I'll eat this now and eat less tomorrow. That's totally doable.*

It may well be true that it's your birthday or that you worked hard. But not everybody eats cake on their birthday and not every treat needs to be food. Even as we say these things to ourselves (or others), we know we're justifying our behavior. We know what we are about to do is not in our best interest, not if we want to be free of addiction and its consequences.

29
SELF-SABOTAGE: EXCUSES

We also use excuses (we often call them *explanations*) to justify our behavior.

- *I had a bad cold so I needed to have ice cream.*
- *I had a tough day at work so I stopped and got corn chips on the way home.*
- *It was my grandson's birthday and I couldn't insult his mother by not eating cake.*

These excuses become foundational in why we aren't succeeding at whatever we want to be doing (losing weight, staying abstinent) but they don't help us change. In fact, they keep us stuck.

Why? Because the cause and effect (head cold = ice cream) isn't nearly that simple. It's completely possible to have a head cold and not eat ice cream. Millions of people do that. The truth is that as addicts, we want to relapse. We want to keep eating and using food to make ourselves feel better (even if, paradoxically, it makes us feel worse). The truth is our addict brains are looking for excuses, looking for justifications. Why? Because a big part of us doesn't really want to change. We don't want to own the fact that we are powerless over those addictive substances and so we blame our circumstances. While this is very human, it is not helpful.

When we argue for our limitations, we get to keep them.
—Evelyn Waugh

30
RECOGNIZING AND SHIFTING OUR SELF-SABOTAGE

An intimate form of self-sabotage can occur for us when we get into recovery. It's subtle and requires us to be conscious of our choices.

It can occur in our behaviors. We continue to drive by that bakery on the way to work in the morning. We invite our best friend to join us for dinner at that restaurant with the fabulous caramel pecan pie. We don't tell our extended family that we've sworn off sugar and flour when we agree to a family event where demon foods will undoubtedly show up on the table.

Self-sabotage can occur in our thoughts and our words. We focus on the cravings, the loss of familiar pleasures, the stresses, the negative experiences of weight loss. That's what we think about. That's what we talk about. We rail against the unfairness of it all, that we can't just eat whatever we want when we want it with no consequences, which is every addict's dream. We stay focused on what we're giving up.

The solution is to shift our perspective to what we're gaining. To think and talk about that. Better health. More flexibility in body. Peace of mind. Freedom.

A friend asked me recently, "So you're never going to eat sugar again?"

"Not if I'm wise," I told her.

"That's awful," she said.

"No," I said. "I get to be free of addiction instead."

31
RECOVERY HELPS US CHANGE OUR RELATIONSHIP WITH THE PAST

In active addiction, we live from an odd and irrational place. *I just ate a piece of candy. Guess I should eat the whole bag.* Or we think *I binged today so I'll wait until the first of the month to stop.* And because we do try to stop and repeatedly fail at it, we assume that we are stuck forever. That what has been true in the past will be true in the future.

With food, we don't always know what will trigger us into overeating. We don't always know what will reactivate the vicious cycle of craving and indulging and self-loathing. And it usually feels so right in the moment. There was such a feeling of relief when I'd buy a bag of soft caramels or a couple of cans of whipped cream to go on whatever. There was such a relief when I had a stash. There was such a strong sense of protection and security involved in that, that it was very hard to see that self-protection as wrong. And that would override my rational beliefs in healthy eating. It seemed far more important to take care of myself emotionally than to take care of myself physically so my 9-year-old self would be in charge and my adult self would cave in to her impulses.

But we can learn to do it differently. We can acknowledge the cravings when they come and do nothing about them. I can stop before I go down the demon foods aisle at the supermarket. I can let the disappointment wash over me at a family dinner when everyone else is eating hot blackberry pie and ice cream. I can sit with boredom and restlessness and befriend them. It means doing nothing, nothing that will harm me in the long run even if it promises to help me in the short run.

Recovery teaches us that it is possible to stop being actively addicted, to stop letting our cravings for sugar and flour run our lives. Will it be easy? Probably not. We will have to let go of our excuses. But is it possible? Absolutely. Our past does not have to be our future.

32
GETTING OUT OF THE SELF-SABOTAGE LOOP

So how do we get out of the excuse loop, out of justifying our behavior, behavior we say we don't want, and out of blaming our circumstances? We have to take our power back and use it for what we want, not for more of the same but for the difference that we're trying to create in our lives. Blaming circumstances is abdicating our power to choose. And of course, choice only exists in the present moment. So we have to pay attention to how we're feeling and what's happening around us.

There are many situations and circumstances that we can't control, but we can control how we respond to them. I'm not telling you anything you haven't heard six dozen times before. But for those of us seeking recovery from addiction, for relief from a well-worn habitual groove in our responses (like eating, drinking, drugging, gambling), we can't afford to not pay attention. We have to assume that we are response-able in each of our circumstances to make choices that support us.

Entitlements, excuses, and justifications are the enemy of effective action. When we fall back on them, we abdicate responsibility for the outcomes in our lives, outcomes we say we want. We have to let go of excuses and explanations and do what we say we will so we can have what we say we want.

FOOD FOR THOUGHT

27 What entitlements are keeping you eating addictively?

28 What justifications keep you relapsing?

29 What excuses are keeping you in active addiction?

30 What self-sabotaging behaviors are keeping you stuck?

31 What has been your experience of repeating your past? What one step towards a different future could you make right now?

32 Where are you irresponsible with food and how does that contradict what you say you want for your body and your health?

33
UNCONSCIOUS SABOTAGE FROM FRIENDS

Most people don't understand addiction. They don't understand that in recovery, the lines we must draw around what we need to eat or not eat and when and how we eat can be very strict. Normal eaters often have a casual attitude about food. Whatever, whenever. But that doesn't work for us.

So when I say I don't eat certain things, it doesn't register with them. And because I don't have life-threatening allergies—they would never offer me a peanut butter cookie if I was allergic to peanuts—they don't take my food restrictions seriously. I've shown up for dinner at a friend's home after responding to "anything you don't eat?—Yes, flour and sugar" and found there to be flour in some form in almost every dish, including croutons in the salad. Then things get awkward. Do I stick to my self-imposed restrictions and deal with a distraught hostess who forgot? Or do I let it go and eat what isn't good for me? My favorite solution for this is to participate primarily in potlucks where I can take a dish I can eat and eat mostly that and push a small quantity of the hostess's dish around on my plate or to eat out at a restaurant where I know I can get what I need.

I do regular writing retreats and volunteer to organize the cooking schedule. I ask the others to keep the meals simple: no sugar, no flour, yes to naked meat/fish, lots of veggies and fruit and serve anything else on the side. Those instructions seem so clear to me but inevitably somebody fixes breaded pork chops or uses sweetened yogurt to sauce the fruit. And I get it. My concerns are not their concerns. So I have to watch out for myself. I'm the one who has to be in charge of what goes on my plate and in my mouth.

34
UNCONSCIOUS SABOTAGE FROM FAMILY

Our families can also be problematic. We may have a spouse who is also addicted to sugar and flour or who is a normal eater but wants dessert every night or candy at the ready. If we live with other food addicts, they may not take kindly to our attempts to change. It will make them nervous to see us succeed at something they know they should be doing too but don't want to.

There are a fair number of folks I know who just don't want to change. They don't want to give up pizza, cheese, French bread, pasta even though they don't feel very good and know they need to lose several dozen pounds or more. But they've tried diets, found them painful and unsuccessful, and they've given up. Because they know they should eat better themselves, they can become food pushers. "One piece of pie won't hurt you. You can burn it off tomorrow."

I grew up in a family with elephantine memories for food. Remember that fried chicken from 1956? That peach pie from 1975 in the backyard at Charlie's house? Those French fries at the Pelican Pub eight years ago? Our birthday and holiday celebrations have always been food-centered: croissant French toast, brie and salmon baked eggs, German chocolate cake, blackberry pie. There isn't a lot of support for change there. It's a tough environment to be in for a recovering food addict.

My family is no stranger to addiction and not just my forms of addiction. Two of us are recovering alcoholics, we all have food issues and are constantly "adjusting" what we eat, we are all workaholics. But traditions and family culture are strong, and we come from a highly disciplined family; two of my siblings have dealt with their addictive tendencies through discipline and will power. And that doesn't work so well for me. That leaves it up to me to say no to the hot blackberry pie and ice cream, the cake, the bread and cheese, and eat my salad by myself. Sometimes I have found that really lonely. My family has been supportive of whatever I want to eat, but they don't really understand how difficult their own eating preferences can be for me some times.

However, since one of my sisters got into recovery for her food issues, it's been a lot easier as we support each other at family gatherings. Having a family food buddy is a huge blessing for me.

35
HEALTH PROFESSIONALS MAY NOT BE HELP PROFESSIONALS

In my experience, most healthcare professionals and even weight loss professionals are not equipped to deal with the complex emotional issues of addiction. Here are three of my experiences.

Last year, concerned by my blood glucose numbers, which were inching ever upward, my doctor sent me to talk to the clinic's diabetes specialist. She was a stick-thin, humorless woman who pulled out plastic plates and plastic foods to show me about portion control. She didn't ask about my concerns or even my eating habits. She had a rehearsed speech and wanted to give it to me. When I asked her if she had diabetes, she said no. When I asked her for help with food addiction, she changed the subject. My own ambivalence about how I was eating threw me into a shame spiral and I just listened politely to her speech and threw all the materials she gave me into the recycling bin on the way out of the office.

Some years before that, I attended Weight Watchers for several months. I was still unable to accept my food addiction and I focused, like so many of us do, on my weight. As I said earlier, some of my family had successful dieting experiences with Weight Watchers so I thought it might work for me. However, from the get-go, I refused the public weighing and told the membership volunteer that if that was a requirement, I wasn't joining. She got permission to let me in anyway. By then, I had been in 12 Steps for a dozen years or so and I had pretty high standards for support meetings. But I was able to set that aside and appreciate the formula of support WW was providing. Until one day.

The discussion topic was dieting in childhood. Dozens of hands went up to speak and several people began to cry. Clearly, the facilitator had touched a nerve with many. Three people shared tearful stories and lots of people nodded their heads. The room had grown somber with pain. More hands went up but in a bright, cheery, artificial voice, the leader, a thin woman in a power suit, said, "Okay, next on the agenda is an announcement about membership discounts." While I could appreciate that she had an agenda she was required to follow, her lack of any recognition of the suffering in the room stunned and angered me, and I never went back.

On a trip to the Caribbean, I met two women physicians fresh out of medical school in Washington, DC. When I asked what they'd been taught about addiction, they said there'd been one afternoon lecture about it in their four years. One lecture! Want to bet that food addiction wasn't even mentioned?

36
SOME REASONS HEALTH PROFESSIONALS MAY NOT BE SO HELPFUL

Most people in our culture do not take addiction seriously, even the well educated. But why should they? They don't have it. Statistically, about 10% of us do. The other 90% can only have an intellectual understanding. Even if they have suffered because of someone else's addiction, they still can't fully grasp it. They can't be in our shoes. This includes a lot of folks working in weight loss. It's no wonder that the focus of many weight-loss professionals is on the physical body. Calories consumed, calories worked off. The biology and chemistry of eating certain foods with other foods (food combining). Protein shakes. Pills to change your metabolism. Surgery to change the mechanics of your digestive system. It's what they know.

There's another reason for the focus on the physiological by professionals. The mechanical aspects of eating and storing fat are so much easier to think about, so much easier to measure, and contemporary science is all about measuring. Calories can be counted. Food interactions can be measured. But our emotional needs to eat? Our trauma, our loneliness, our dissatisfaction? Those are very hard to measure. They aren't objective. They aren't numerical or easily sorted out. So while a physiology focus works well for researchers in our mechanistic society, it doesn't help us addicts get into recovery and stay there.

37
CULTURAL SABOTAGE: FOOD FOR PROFIT

The ways of eating that work for recovery from food addiction are counter-cultural. A huge percentage of our population eats mostly crap: fast food, junk food, sodas, candy. A few folks may not know that this stuff is lethal, but most folks do know, I think. Yet many can't afford better food, and even more are seduced by the food industry's diligent efforts to create hyper-palatable foods with a lot of fat, salt, and sugar.

The restaurant corporations and grocery corporations want to get us hooked on those foods so we will buy more, and most of us do get hooked. Foods with chemicals have a longer shelf-life than fresh foods, and processed foods are a huge industry in our culture. These foods are, by design, meant to be so delicious that you will buy them again and again and again. Restaurants, grocery stores, and processed food manufacturers do not have your best interests at heart; they are concerned with their bottom lines, not our waist lines. While weight loss programs are a huge industry, the get-us-fat programs are even bigger and government-sanctioned through subsidies.

There's a second big group of folks who eat better but are still living by the eating ideas we grew up, even though the Food Pyramid shifted years ago away from meat and dairy and refined grains and sugar. But the meat and dairy and wheat associations are also huge, powerful lobbies that have big agribusiness money behind them for advertising. (You never hear about the vegetable growers as lobbyists.) Big business isn't much interested in the precious perishables and not much interested at all in giving up GMOs and herbicides and pesticides that make food easy to store and ship.

These forms of cultural sabotage impact us every day.

38
MORE ON FOOD FOR PROFIT

One influential source of information for me was David Kessler's *The End of Overeating*. Kessler is a former US Surgeon General who set out to understand why he always bought two huge chocolate chip cookies and then obsessed about them until he had eaten them both. While he does talk some about addiction and the inner workings that lead to our food obsession, he spends a lot more time talking about the food industry and how they have shaped our cravings and our palates to lust after salt, sugar, and fat.

I won't go into the details here (his book is very accessible and well worth reading), but our mouths basically become addicted to salty, sugary, smooth foods that don't take much chewing. Those foods just slide on down, much to the delight of our mouths and the delight of the restaurant owners, who get us to come back and do it again. How food tastes is being manipulated for profit reasons. It's not illegal, and it may not even be immoral. It's up to us consumers to know what we're getting and if that's what we want.

Those industries are aided and abetted by the very foundation of our consumer culture. Michael Pollan is a food sociologist, I guess you could say, and in his book *Cooked*, one sentence struck me so much, I copied it down. In our culture, Pollan says, "The only legitimate form of leisure is consumption." The fact that Pollan is talking about this in a book focused on the kitchen means he's also talking about food.

Consuming food is an enormous part of our leisure. Many of us eat when we get together with friends: coffee and a scone, dessert, tea and a cookie, meeting over lunch, over dinner. I know I did. If we go to sports events, we eat. If we go hiking, we take food. We eat in our cars, in our beds, in front of the TV. I live in a small city with an astounding number of restaurants, many of them full every night. We seem to have lost our interest in most activities that don't involve food. At the same time, we seldom just eat. We read and eat, talk and eat, watch TV and eat. So it isn't really just about the food. It's about consuming, whether we're alone or with others. This is not good news for those of us who are addicted to food.

39
FOOD ADDICTION AND THE TV

You may know the name of the Russian physiologist Ivan Pavlov, who initiated the concept of conditioned responses. He fed dogs and rang a bell at the same time. Before too long, the dogs would salivate at the sound of the bell even when no food was present. I have had a Pavlovian relationship with TV. For decades, I've eaten in front of the TV, mostly mindlessly. A great deal of the extra weight I carry is from TV eating. TV eating is seldom about hunger. It's about restlessness, it's about loneliness, and it's definitely about conditioning. Yet my emotional self struggles with giving this up. She keeps saying, "We'll suffer if you do that. We won't make it."

Snacking in front of the TV is an all-American pastime and not doing this seems counter-cultural, radical, revolutionary, and worst of all, restrictive. But doing so is a sure-fire way to stay in addiction. And there's more:

- Extra calories that add up to more than we need in a day.
- Extra calories that don't get burned while we sleep so they add up to extra pounds (or less weight loss).
- Disturbed sleep. Many foods stimulate the third-eye chakra (intuition, visions) giving us weird dreams and making us feel that we've been busy all night.
- We don't physically rest as well since our digestive system has to digest (digesting means less resting).

Maybe you don't eat while you watch TV. Maybe you eat while you read a mystery or a romance. Maybe it's that combination that is the most soothing to you. Maybe you eat while you surf the Internet or maybe you eat out of a drawer in your desk at work or on every coffee break during the work day. We all have our patterns, our Pavlovian routines. This is part of the environment that has to change if we are to find recovery from food addiction.

FOOD FOR THOUGHT

33 How have you let others' encouragement or pressures sabotage your intentions to be in recovery from food addiction?

34 How do your family relationships play out in your food addiction issues?

35-36 What has been your experience with health professionals and your food addiction?

37 In what ways besides food are you addicted to consuming?

38 When and where do you eat? How does this contribute to your food addiction?

39 What is your relationship with eating and TV?

"Today I had my green smoothie, some oatmeal, and a big salad with turkey but I ate dinner early, about 5, because I was really hungry and then I was still hungry and I ate some nuts and that held me for a while and then I was hungry again. And rather than sit with it or have a big glass of water, I fixed another snack. Half an avocado and salsa and chips and I ate too much of it. I was watching TV and I just kept eating. I didn't even think of my commitment or my intention or anything. I wasn't thinking, I was just eating."

—From my journal

40
CULTURAL SABOTAGE: LIVING IN A LAND OBSESSED WITH THIN

We live in a culture where what you weigh is not a private matter. Instead of being concerned about how fit and healthy we are, our culture is concerned with how thin we are, especially if we're female. Our food industry makes the food irresistible, our consuming culture—often including our friends and family—encourages us to eat, and at the same time, we are demeaned, bullied, and badgered for weight gain. As food addicts, we often respond to demeaning, bullying, and badgering by eating more.

In a sense, I think this is another part of our Puritan heritage with its loathing of the physical body. Our culture has long had a narrow view of sexuality and sensuality. These inclinations to wrap the body in morality extend to how much we eat. Our compulsive eating habits, like other addictions, are seen as moral failures. If only we had the self-discipline, we wouldn't eat like this, we wouldn't gain all this weight. If only we took better care of ourselves, we wouldn't eat like this, we'd stay thin. Never mind that in compulsively eating, we are taking care of ourselves the best way we know how. The moral judges don't see that; they don't offer us emotional solutions, just criticism. Yet it is emotional solutions we need.

41
AND THEN THERE ARE THE HOLIDAY LANDMINES

Family and culture collide at Thanksgiving, at Christmas, at New Year's—potential disasters for the food addict. Since we have become a culture that indulges and overindulges all the time, you'd think that holiday groaning boards would be no big deal. But because we often bring our old emotional baggage around the holidays down from the attic or up from the basement to drag around at gatherings, we are even more susceptible.

What's more, many of us have unrealistic expectations of happiness and joy at the holidays, as if our family issues will all disappear or we will suddenly have that fabulous life partner so we won't be lonely anymore. The truth is many of us are lonely at the holidays, no matter how many gatherings we attend. We grieve family and friends who have passed on, we grieve our divorces, our estrangements from children or siblings or friends. So we drown our feelings in dip and punch and cake and candy. The holidays can be a tough time for anyone and they are often particularly difficult for addicts.

All of these cultural and familial obstacles encourage us to succumb to what I call the *Power of Not Now*. I will stop overeating after the holidays, after my birthday, next Monday, on the first of the month, just not now. *Not now* is seductive when you are trying to change a habit that you don't really want to change. *Not now* is especially powerful when the reason you don't really want to change has to do with your feelings and your dissatisfaction with your life.

42
ENVIRONMENTAL SABOTAGE

An obesity epidemic like the one I've been participating in is only possible in a culture of plenty. There has to be plenty of food available to overeat. And we have plenty of food available. Need sweets? There's a convenience store on every other corner or a little market. You can buy your sugar or flour drug of choice at a gas station, coffee shop, grocery store, vending machine. At the airport, at the office. We can eat all the time and many of us do.

As mentioned earlier, most of us spend our leisure time consuming. We consume TV, we consume video games, we consume goods (clothes, books, cars, toys, music). We are a consumer society. And we are a society of excess. As a culture, we encourage over-working, over-playing, over-spending, over-consuming, over-eating. More is always better—until it kills us. You don't need me to tell you about the statistics of the obesity epidemic. I'm one of those statistics. You may be as well.

When I got sober, I found it easy to avoid being in the presence of alcohol. I just didn't go to bars and taverns and liquor stores. I avoided the wine and beer aisle at the grocery store like the plague. I can also keep my home environment safe from demon foods with sugar, fat, and flour. But the outside world is full of it. It is no wonder that in addition to our own personal demons, we struggle with sabotage from the world around us.

FOOD FOR THOUGHT

40 How has our cultural obsession with thin impacted you?

41 How does the power of *Not Now* play out in your life with food?

42 Where do trigger foods show up in your environment? What is your relationship with junk food?

HOW SOOTHING OURSELVES IS THE REAL PROBLEM

43
THE PARADOX OF TAKING CARE OF OURSELVES

It's one of the ironies of active addiction that we are destroying ourselves by trying to take care of ourselves. While a few emotionally healthy people may fall into addiction as a result of pure pleasure-seeking, nearly all of us come into food and other addictions trying to relieve the pressure of negative feelings. We've experienced emotional or physical or sexual trauma. We've been abandoned or neglected or bullied. We've internalized a lot of shame and had our self-esteem badly damaged. We are looking for ways to feel better and we use whatever is available.

The sad thing about addictive substances is that they work. They do make us feel better. After a hard day at elementary school, I could eat six pieces of toast with butter and jam and be okay to be at home. I could eat candy during the day at school and my anxiety, restlessness, and boredom would lessen. I didn't know I was medicating myself. I just knew I had to have something to feel better. I was taking care of myself the best way I knew how.

And I've gone on doing that all of my life. I ate sweets and fat foods to feel better. Then I drank to take the edge off my life so I could feel better. When I got sober, I went back to sweets to take care of myself.

Now I can see that taking care of myself that way was a destructive choice. It didn't feel destructive in the moment. It felt right. But addiction turns on us. The help begins to disappear and the hurt starts happening. The physical consequences begin to outweigh the relief, and we have to find healthier ways to care for ourselves.

44
WHEN THE SOLUTION BECOMES THE PROBLEM

Compulsive consuming is a particularly easy solution to many kinds of personal dilemmas in our culture with its overabundance of consumables. At an early age we begin soothing ourselves by medicating with food, with alcohol, with drugs. We bury the original trauma as deep as we can. Even when we become aware of it, we know that the past cannot be undone, that there is no curing that problem, so we resolve it the best way we've learned how.

My 9-year-old self didn't know she had the genetics for addiction. She just knew she got relief from candy. And as she grew up, she went on taking care of herself the same way, adding alcohol and codependent relationships to the soothers. At a certain point, the solution becomes its own problem although we can be caught for years or decades or our whole lives, as it takes a long time to see the shift from solution to problem. What's more, we grow used to having the problem. We become wedded to it. We may even cling to it as if our lives depend on it.

It's not just the pleasure of the food that we don't want to lose. Many of us don't even taste the food after the first bite or two. Instead, we cling to eating as the problem because it is easier to have that problem than face our real issues: childhood trauma or neglect, adolescent humiliations, adult disappointments and losses, the suffering of life. The devil we know seems easier than the devil we imagine. It seems easier to me to struggle with food and weight and health issues than it does to struggle with chronic anxiety and fear. Who wants that? And just as I couldn't imagine a life without alcohol before I got sober, I had a hard time imagining there is a way to not be chronically anxious and afraid. I still do. I have had an even more difficult time imagining having no major problem at all.

In addition, we addicts identify with our problems. They become how we relate to the world. I'm many things: a former college professor, a speaker of French, an editor, a sister, a daughter, a great friend, a painter, a published writer, a novelist, an artist, a creative. But when

I'm active in my addiction, none of that is me. My identity boils down to compulsive eater. That runs the show.

When this goes on long enough, the other parts of who we are get eclipsed and this becomes the filter for everything. It becomes our mask, our costume, the container we live in. In a very real sense, it becomes our identity. By this, I don't mean the label someone else gives to us. I mean it becomes the essence of who we are to ourselves. In many ways, what other people think of us is minor. It's painful if they say it out loud, but it's no more painful than how we relate to ourselves. Self-loathing is a terrible experience.

45
STRESS AND TRAUMA ARE MY PROBLEM, NOT FOOD

It didn't take my PhD for me to figure out that I started eating compulsively right after I got sober so that I wouldn't have to deal with my feelings. Being newly sober was terrifying. I felt raw and exposed to a world that I had perceived only dimly through the filter of an alcoholic haze. And once those first painful months passed, I kept on eating. I had broken up with my partner of 10 years and had no clue how to have a romantic or sexual relationship without alcohol. I was vaguely aware that I kept on eating so that I wouldn't have to deal with some of the potential complications of dating and intimacy.

Eating a lot of fat and sugar (aka ice cream) was also a sensual substitute for sex and affection, and since our cultural ideal is a thin woman, I just removed myself from the playing field pound by pound. I couldn't stand feeling such vulnerability, and I didn't have the courage to face it so I ate and ate and ate.

There were other feelings I was trying to avoid as well. I was still numbing myself from the pain and trauma of my childhood. I had done years of talk therapy around those issues, but I had never had the courage to feel them, to heal that part of myself that wasn't mothered very well, the part that longs to be held and touched and is so afraid. This is the part of myself that I so often have turned away from. The wounded child, the needy, dependent self, who is at the same time reaching out to connect and running away in fear and distrust. This is the me I drank to escape. This is the me I kept eating too much and working too much to escape.

In an interesting book called *Unchain Your Brain*, two MDs looked at the brain chemistry of addiction both from a physiological model and a psychological model. I was struck in particular by their division of addicts into 6 types: compulsive, impulsive, compulsive-impulsive, sad/emotional, temporal lobe (aka rage-aholics), and anxious. I fit perfectly into the anxious category (too much cortisol and too much worry). It also didn't surprise me to learn that food addiction is most common in my group for we are looking for anything and everything to soothe us. Because our anxiety is chronic, we usually hoard our soothers of choice so that we always have a supply, rather than running out and having to go out to get some when we are out. That explained a lot of my behavior to me.

46
MY VERSION OF FOOD INSECURITY

Food insecurity usually refers to people who don't know where their next meal is coming from. I suffer from a different form of this insecurity. I buy way more than I need, way more than I can eat; among the emotional components of my type of addiction is the need to have food—plenty of choices and plenty of quantity—available to me. I do not like being hungry. It makes me anxious, it makes me panicky. So I shop as if I am headed to the hinterlands where nothing will be available and not just a few blocks down the street. I shop as if a lot of food can save me.

In keeping with the wisdom of the mid-1940s, I was bottle-fed and I was fed on a schedule. Mothers were admonished back then to feed their babies every four hours regardless of what the baby wanted. I don't know if this was for convenience or a sense of discipline or trying to move us to three meals a day from the get-go. But I suspect I was hungry a lot and that it created some kind of survival anxiety in me. Many of my age peers talk of having the same relationship with food.

Being an anxious addict also explains to me why I don't enjoy the food I'm eating compulsively. I'm not interested in the food itself or what it tastes like. I'm only interested in being soothed, and I've identified certain foods that do that pretty quickly. In other words, I want alcohol, sugar, and fat to take me away from where I am into some place more tolerable. I started to say "more pleasant" but I'm not sure that's it. It's more like a miserable itch. It may be painful to scratch it but it's better than the itch itself.

FOOD FOR THOUGHT

43 How is your food addiction a result of taking care of yourself?

44 How do you identify with your food addiction as a problem?

45 What is food helping you run away from?

46 Does food insecurity affect you? Give an example or two if it does.

47
EATING TO SOOTHE OURSELVES

Some time ago, I heard a woman at a 12-Step meeting talk about her several relapses with alcohol. She'd had a couple of surgeries and a lot of pain, but that hadn't been the cause of her relapsing. She'd had a death in her family but had stayed sober. Instead, each time she'd started drinking again, it was because of plain, old life discomfort: anxiety, nervousness, general malaise. She just didn't want to feel bad. The old admonition to sit with your feelings, to sit with discomfort was something she couldn't do.

I felt such empathy for her. This same inability to be with discomfort was certainly why I started drinking and probably why I kept on drinking for so long. I didn't want to be uneasy, or jealous, or anxious, or off-kilter. But then I crossed some physiological line and alcohol didn't work anymore to numb my feelings. It just made me sick. So when I got sober, I turned to other soothers. Work soothes me, eating soothes me, shopping can soothe me. Not everything that soothes me is bad, but that intolerance for discomfort is a tough one for me to handle, to understand, to sit with.

In David Krueger's *The Secret Language of Money*, he talks about a great deal more than money. He's interested in how we do life, what we expect and don't expect, and he uses money as a medium of discussion. Of course, he talks some about addictions around money: spending addiction, debt, gambling. But he also talks at length about the restlessness of addiction. The dopamine rush we get from spending whether it's cash or credit card, online or in person, and how we want more of that rush. Always more. All of what he says, of course, also applies to food, in fact, to any of those things that some of us do in such excess. And here's the sentence that really blew me away: "When one is addicted to something, the hardest thing to do is nothing."

That is my lived experience. I think of it as the inability to stop doing something, stop drinking, stop eating, stop working so hard, but it's really an inability to do nothing. To just sit there or stand there or lie there until the need, the restlessness, the agitation passes. I have spent most of my life going from one soother to another. To do nothing in the face of discomfort has seemed impossible.

48
EATING TO ESCAPE HYPER-VIGILANCE

Some of my resistance to doing nothing when the cravings come has to do with vigilance. After my weeks sleeping in fear across the road when I was 9, I became hyper-vigilant, acutely attuned to my environment, always watching, always calculating to be sure that I was safe. Some of my hyper-vigilance had to do with the external environment: my teachers' reactions, my mother's moods, the world at large, which was filled with murderers and rapists and accidents and illness, all things *out there* that I had to guard against.

At the same time, I also had to guard against my inner environment. The nightmares, the panic, the throat and chest and stomach that would get jittery or achy or painful with no warning. Wanting so much for someone to hold me, to make it all better, and knowing that that was never going to happen. Ever.

Once I got sober, some of the hyper-vigilance eased up. But the underlying anxiety and fear and anger never went away, never got expressed, and when I tried to restrict food, it would all bubble up and threaten to drown me and I would just go back to eating, to keeping those feelings down.

One characteristic of many addicts is that we have a very limited repertoire of soothers, of ways that we can take care of ourselves emotionally. This is where the obsession comes in. I get into a certain psychic space and I can't see my way out except in one direction: eat the current soother—the Dove Bars, the caramels, the ice cream sandwiches, the toffee peanuts—whatever I'm currently focused on.

I'm unsure what creates this mono-focus. Perhaps it's as simple and complex as that well-worn groove in my brain that has so closely interwoven emotional distress and food so that nothing else is available. As I discussed earlier, new neural pathways, new grooves can be laid down and the old grooves can die off from disuse. Over the many years of my sobriety, I've proven that the cravings and need for alcohol can wither and fade away. But when I'm in the grip of discomfort and craving around food, I find that experience hard to remember.

49
EATING TO BELONG

Many of us also eat to belong. My family doesn't all watch sports, and we don't play sports. We don't camp or hike much or hunt or fish. We read a lot and play cards. But mostly we eat together. It's what we do. My sister Kerry is an amazing pie maker. She also is a cake connoisseur. Our adopted sister Melanie is just this side of a master chef. She's got Paula Deen's decadent French toast down. Several of us are at a healthy weight; several of us are not. But eating and enjoying what we eat and talking about what we eat and what we have eaten in the past is a huge part of our life together.

In food recovery, eating with my family can be difficult. Occasionally I feel virtuous, disciplined, committed, but mostly I feel lonely and sad. My old yearnings get stirred, not for the foods themselves, but for the nonchalance of eating whatever I want without thinking about ingredients. I miss being heedless, thinking only about the enjoyment of my mouth and not the health of my body.

When I talked to a good friend about this, she wrote back: "I wonder if this desire to eat what's put out to share at a family or friend meal isn't a throw back to being part of the Tribe, a way to identify deeply with the other bodies we share so much of everything else with, including love." This struck a deep chord with me.

Sitting at a table where everyone else is exclaiming about how delicious something is and enjoying the communal experience while I push lettuce leaves around is painful sometimes. In an instant, I am that deeply lonely 10-year-old, 14-year-old, 20-year-old who didn't get asked to play or to dance, who's on the outside looking in while everyone else has a good time. While healthier foods will satisfy my physical hunger, they do not always seem to satisfy the hunger to belong.

Recently I was having a meal with friends. All the foods on the table were safe foods for me: a veggie curry, cucumber salad, melon. And I filled my plate and enjoyed my food. But as the time wore on, I watched others continuing to eat: more nuts, more melon, and I began to do the same. It wasn't until I got up and moved away from the table that I could stop. There was no pressure from any of them for me to continue eating, but I had felt an internal pressure to do so, to be part of the group. I thought of my friend's idea about the Tribe.

50
EATING AND THE INNER CHILD

It's well known to most addiction counselors that addiction most often brings an arrested emotional development. We start using alcohol, drugs, sugar, food to mask our insecurities and fears and because we don't deal with those feelings, those feelings wait inside us. Over many years of therapy and counseling and all kinds of ritual work, I have come to know the stuck places in me: the infant who didn't get enough loving attention, the terrified 9-year-old, the 14-year-old who had no one to talk to about her awkwardness and her sexual desires, the 22-year-old desperate for love and using her body to get it. I could see that these were places where I stopped developing in a healthy way, places that remained unhealed.

Over the last 9 years I've worked with a wonderful counselor who incorporates these inner selves into her work, helping people move them from mental concepts about them to experiences we can feel in the body. This work has been very difficult and I've met it with a lot of resistance. I sense there is such a depth of anger and sorrow and fear in there that I'm afraid I won't survive.

Some months ago I was talking with her about how I felt such overwhelming resistance to suggestions to plan out my food and eat on a schedule, and I started to cry. After a minute, she asked me how old the self was who was resisting and I thought for a moment and then said 8 or 9.

"Perhaps your child self only knows how to get in touch with you through hunger," she said. "It certainly seems to get your attention."

"What does?"

"Hunger," she said. "Or what feels like hunger."

And I realized that while I'm willing to admit there's an emotional component to some of my hunger feelings, I've always assumed it was my adult self that was bored or restless. It hadn't really occurred to me that it was a sad and lonely little girl who needed attention and could only fix it for herself by eating toast with butter and sugar or candy bars.

FOOD FOR THOUGHT

47 Do you eat to soothe yourself? What kind of experiences trigger this need for soothing?

48 What kinds of feelings are you eating to avoid?

49 Do you ever eat to belong? What circumstances trigger this?

50 Are you aware of younger parts of yourself that have a role in your food addiction?

51
GIVING OURSELVES ATTENTION RATHER THAN FOOD

I've known about the idea of the inner child since I read Wayne Muller's wonderful *The Spiritual Advantages of a Painful Childhood*. I've done shamanic journeys to reintegrate these parts of myself and done inner-child workshops and retreats. However, those unhappy inner selves are still running the show an awful lot of the time.

My inner 9-year-old is a sad and lonely self who grew up too fast when there was no one to comfort her. Food was her soother, her savior. My inner 14-year-old is an angry adolescent who feels unseen, unheard, unloved. And why shouldn't she? I didn't love myself at 14: gawky, too tall, too thin, unlovely, ungraceful. I was mistrusting of adults who only seemed to like me when I was smart and dutiful. I was awkward around my peers, some of whom made fun of me.

We all have these stories. My guess is that inside most compulsive eaters is a deeply wounded child. But knowing about them and caring for them are two different things.

If what my therapist says is true, that hunger may be the only way these parts of myself can get my attention, then those impulses of restlessness, boredom, a vague sadness unrelated to present circumstances, each of those impulses that I respond to with a candy bar or a dish of ice cream may well be me wanting me to pay attention, to be present in a different way.

And I think about how I seldom have time for my inner self even though I have plenty of time for Netflix and reading and shopping and working. And I bypass meditation and contemplation, sitting quietly, the best way to learn to pay attention. And instead of loving those victims, those survivors within myself, I have given them sweets to shut them up. What would happen if I listen instead? Me paying attention, me listening to what I'm trying to tell myself, me loving myself.

52
THEN THERE'S SHAME...

There is, I think, a special relationship that we addicts have with shame and fear and guilt, the triumvirate of yuck. For nearly two decades I felt ashamed of my drinking, guilty for the lies I told, afraid that I was killing myself. Then I got sober and for a few years, I didn't have those three malevolent stooges in my head anymore.

But after about five years of consistent candy consumption, I was deeply hooked into sugar addiction, and I expanded my horizons and became thoroughly habituated to using all kinds of food as sedative. And as I put the weight on and then more weight, as I ate a lot of fat and sugar and salt, I felt out of control (shame), worried about my health (fear), and angry that I couldn't stop myself (guilt). And the Larry, Moe, and Curly of emotions came back from their extended vacation and took up residence again.

The sad truth is that shame and self-loathing don't motivate us to change our behavior, to stop drinking or eating compulsively. In fact, the opposite is true. They motivate us to self-medicate with the same substance that creates the shame. It's a terrible, self-perpetuating cycle that we must break if we are to recover.

53
...AND THE FEAR OF HAPPINESS

We are also, many of us, afraid to be happy. A good friend and I were talking recently about where we are stuck in our old stories and old beliefs. We talked about the energy it takes to move out of the unpleasant but comfortable and risk something new. I've done so much personal work that sometimes I get the feeling I should have made much more progress by now than I have. I should have the sugar addiction resolved by this point. Why do I eat as if there's no tomorrow when I say I want to lose weight and feel lighter and freer in my body? Why do I eat sugar when I say I want to be abstinent? Why do I have to talk about things for such a long time and so repeatedly before I'm willing?

Because I don't trust happiness. If you're not an addict, this may seem crazy. But many of us addicts are afraid to be happy. Of course, that makes no sense. Why wouldn't we want to feel good? Everybody wants to feel good. And of course, we do too. But we don't trust it. We saw happiness flip to sadness—or rage—in the blink of an eye. The mother who kissed us goodnight so warmly was angry and curt with us the next morning. The father who was relaxed and playful with one drink was raging an hour later. One of the most effective elements of torture is unpredictability. Deepak Chopra says humans can handle almost anything but that kind of chaos, and I agree.

My mother's moods were mercurial: okay, not okay, cold, sad, aloof, comforting. My father's presence was undependable: he came home most nights late and left early; he had too much energy, I realize now, for the domestic life. The men in my romantic life were similar: either mercurial in their affections or undependable. Of course they were. That was what I knew how to relate to.

And the truth is that happiness doesn't last. But happiness for many of us seems only an invitation to relax, let our guard done, and then wham! We're down again and either disappointed or devastated. Better just to stay down. This is so fundamental to us that we will sabotage ourselves. In the TV show, *Nurse Jackie* relapses on the one-year anniversary of her sobriety. A friend from AA went on the vacation of a lifetime to Italy and was so happy she drank for the first time in 12 years. She drank for another two years after that. Better to reduce the unpredictability in our own lives by clinging to the problem we already have. We know that misery. It is familiar, and in a strange way that is comforting.

    A healthy person would think we'd want to rid ourselves of this terrible identity. There's that rational thinking again. But this identification with our problem is so familiar, so ingrained, that we often don't know how to live without it. I think this may be why so many of us don't stay sober, whether from food or alcohol or drugs or you name it. Being healthy, being happy, that's scary. It can vanish so quickly and probably will. Better to stay with what we know. And yet. Something pulls some of us towards health, towards wholeness.

FOOD FOR THOUGHT

51 What might happen if you gave yourself attention rather than food?

52 How is shame around your weight and your eating keeping you in the addiction?

53 Are you afraid to be happy? How does this keep you stuck in compulsive eating?

None of us is ever able to part with our survival strategies without significant support and the cultivation of replacement strategies.

—Brene Brown, *Daring Greatly*

Part II
THE WAY OUT

WE COMMIT TO CHANGING OUR STORIES

54
HOW OUR STORIES GET US INTO TROUBLE AND HOW THEY CAN SAVE US

We humans are story machines. We are hard-wired to learn from story. It's not just a quaint fact that the earliest peoples told stories of their days, their experiences, their learnings around the fire. They were teaching themselves what they needed to know to survive. They were teaching each other. It's how we learn best. Studies of how college students remember what they read shows that they retain very little of the theory or statistical information but most all of the case studies and examples—the stories.

We tell stories to our friends and family all the time. "Wait 'til you hear what happened to me today." We don't think of them as stories. We think of them as the facts, as what's true in our experience. But they are still stories. They are how we teach each other, how we teach ourselves. It's how we learn.

All of the stories we tell about ourselves, about our experiences, our family, our early environments are in the past, and we carry the learnings forward and they influence how we think and feel and act in the present. Many of these stories are benign and some are joyous. Others, the most difficult, are not benign. They can hold us stuck in what is no longer true but feels like it is.

I've carried some of my stories since I was 9 years old. Here's one: *No one is going to watch out for me except me. If I need something, I have to give it to myself. Other people may care about me, may sometimes be there for me but I can't count on it.* This story came directly from my experience in my family. Here's another: *No one wants to hear about sadness or anger or misery. "If you can say something nice, don't say anything at all." Don't talk about your feelings. In fact, don't feel them. It's just easier.*

Don't Trust and Don't Feel Your Feelings were two perfect companions for my journey into addiction. They led me into fear, anxiety, and restlessness; and stuffing those feelings down with food or drowning them with alcohol seemed the only way out. And while part of these stories were true, my generalizations were not. While my parents weren't reliable, I had a grandmother whom I could have trusted, who would have listened to my feelings, but it never occurred to me to tell her. I had kind teachers too but I was so convinced by my stories that I never ventured into any place of vulnerability.

If we want to recover from food addiction, we have to let our old stories go. We have to uncover them and rewrite them.

55
FINDING THE COURAGE TO GIVE UP OLD DEFENSE MECHANISMS

In a very real sense, the foods we eat compulsively are defense mechanisms. They protect us from emotional pain, from fear and anger and grief. They buffer our existence. Recovery asks us to become willing not only to let go of those substances as defenses but also to let go of any other habits that keep us from showing up and living life fully.

We humans have an intricate array of such defenses. In active addiction, they can play out as pride and arrogance (too independent to ask for help or to use the help that is offered), denial that we even have a problem, anger (which takes us back to pride and arrogance), intellectualism (too smart to have this problem and smart enough to figure it out all by ourselves), passivity (I just can't do anything about this), blame (it's not my fault)—and, my favorite, excuses (if you had my life, you'd eat too). You get the picture.

But I know that for me it all boils down to one thing: fear. I could give you examples of all those traits in me. There are plenty of them. But they're just versions of my fear of being overwhelmed by my feelings, of unbearable emotional pain: all the things that didn't happen that I wanted to have happen, all the things that happened that I didn't want, all the bad choices, all the missed opportunities, all the loneliness, all the sorrow, all the injustice and unfairness of my world and the world at large, all the life as it happens to us.

So when that fear came creeping around my sensitive, tender heart, I checked out with food. I ate until the fear went away. In a very real sense, I ran away although without leaving home. I abandoned myself. It's the one thing I didn't learn from my parents that I really needed. From them, I learned to be responsible, to keep my word, to problem solve, to be a good student, to be a good citizen, to be kind to others, to work hard and do my best. All wonderful things for success in the world. But I didn't learn to face my feelings, to be with them until those feelings could move on through me and be gone. Instead I learned to stuff them down, to eat, to get busy, to pretend they weren't there.

That abandonment, that running away from ourselves, is the defense mechanism we must release if we are to have peace with food.

56
CURIOSITY MAY BE OUR MOST IMPORTANT TOOL

If there's a truth at the heart of this book, if there's a solution, it is this. We need to show up when our feelings come around. Stop and pay attention to them. Acknowledge them, experience them until they are done with us. Give up abandoning ourselves as a defense.

My 120+ extra pounds didn't just represent a lot of candy and ice cream and grilled cheese sandwiches. They also represented a lot of sadness, a lot of fear, a lot of resentment. It was stuck in me and I wanted to release it. But in order to do that, I have to be willing to do nothing. That's right. Nothing.

I have to be willing to not eat when the feelings come. To not get busy at the computer. To not turn on the TV or pick up a novel. To not play solitaire. I have to be willing to let those distraactions go and get curious, as Brene Brown says, about my feelings instead of self-medicating.

If we can get curious about our stories, we can rewrite them. If we can get curious about our feelings, we can survive them. If we can get curious about being fully alive rather than numb, we can recover. We can welcome everything and push away nothing.

57
WORTHINESS DOESN'T HAVE PREREQUISITES

Many food addicts suffer from self-worth issues. We have made up or bought into stories that we aren't enough as we are, that we must continually prove our worth, our right to be here. By *we made up stories*, I mean that we responded to events, often in childhood, by believing we weren't worthy of love because those who brought us up believed they weren't worthy of it either. Sometimes they even told us so and we bought into that. We took it to heart as the truth, and we came to believe that we don't deserve to be happy, to be free of addiction, that suffering is what we deserve. Some religious systems help perpetuate these ideas.

To fully embrace recovery, we have to change this belief. We have to come to believe that joy and contentment and peace of mind are available, that the chaos of our active addiction can be released, and that we can be set free. If we don't address these beliefs, we may well find ourselves sabotaging our recovery.

The 12-Step programs talk about our need to change our "playmates and playgrounds." We can pull away or limit our exposure to friends, family, and coworkers who don't understand abstinence, who continue to offer us demon foods. We can stop going to restaurants or shops that specialize in our trigger foods. Just as recovering alcoholics don't go into bars, food addicts in recovery don't meet friends in bakeries or ice cream shops. We don't do this as punishment for past sins. We do this because we believe in ourselves and the value of our health and well-being. We believe that we deserve peace in our lives and happiness, not just soothing and masking suffering.

We deserve to be happy and free of addiction. It can be a strange idea, one that contradicts what you've always believed, but it's true and something you can fully embrace in recovery.

FOOD FOR THOUGHT

54 What stories from the past are running your addiction?

55 What are you running away from with food?

56 What might you be willing to get curious about in service to your recovery?

57 You are already worthy and deserving of freedom. How does it feel to begin to embrace this idea? What can you do to strengthen this belief for yourself?

58
THE IMPORTANCE OF CHANGING OUR STORIES

A woman I know in food addiction recovery is embarking on a big adventure: six months living on a sailboat with her husband. Heidi was charged with reducing their possessions for storage. As part of the process, she read through 30 years of journals and was appalled to discover how much energy she had given in her life, how many years she'd given, to food obsession. She read through all the diets she had tried, all the weight regained, all the misery. Year after year, it was the same old story.

As a long-time journal-keeper, I can so relate. I haven't read through all my old journals but the rereading I have done has shown the same thing. That year after year, I've been living the same story of giving my power away to food and then alcohol and then food again. Then I get a reprieve from the misery but after a few months, I buy in again, seduced by taste and flavors and the desire to be numb.

Heidi decided she'd had enough. She recognized all the lost time in her life bemoaning her weight and never really committing to her own well-being. She's changing her story about what's important and having faith that she can relate to food and to her body differently. I want this too.

59
CHANGING OUR LIVES HELPS US CHANGE OUR STORIES

Like Heidi, my sister has struggled with her weight as long as I can remember. She didn't inherit the longer, leaner body that I did. She takes after my mom's side of the family: shorter and wider by genetics. She also inherited the gene for addiction and experienced some of the same family trauma that I did. She has tried almost every diet, fast, and commercial solution over the years to lose weight and keep it off, all without success. She became resigned to obesity and bought into the story that it would never change.

However, since last summer (2015), she has lost 84 pounds. She went from a 3x to a 16 in nine months. She hasn't weighed this little in about 50 years. Curiously enough, it isn't the food plan that has made the difference for she's on a modified Atkins plan and she'd done the Atkins plan several times before. So what did she change that made the difference? She changed her life.

She quit a high-paying stressful job as a medical editor that required her to work all night; she was eating all night to stay awake. She walked away from an upside-down mortgage that had her chained to that job; she was eating to numb out from the financial stress. She also ate from loneliness, so she moved out of the city into the country to the vineyard of some close friends. She rents a tiny old house from them and shares meals and chores.

None of this happened overnight of course. It took about a year to make the big changes, a year of openness to changing her life. Since then, weight loss has been possible. Her old life supported addiction. Her new life supports recovery. When our story is faith in recovery, our possibilities are endless.

60
SOME WAYS TO CHANGE OUR STORIES

Like most things that have to do with recovery, a steady process is everything. We may make a firm decision at one moment to stop eating compulsively; in fact, we must at some point do that. But recovery itself is a lifelong process and so is changing our stories. If you can see that you have stories that need changing, here are some ideas to help you get started.

- Use your journal to explore the questions in this book.
- Share your answers to these questions with a therapist, spiritual director, 12-Step sponsor, or trusted friend.
- For each story you uncover, write an alternate version in which you give yourself credit for surviving and you explore the strengths that experience taught you.
- Discuss the questions in this book with friends who also suffer from food or other addictions. There's considerable strength in numbers.
- Uncover more of your stories with the help of a therapist or spiritual director.

61
CHANGING OUR WAY OF THINKING ABOUT FOOD

The purpose of recovery from sugar and food addiction is to feel better, a lot better. We want to eat to empower ourselves rather than just to power through unpleasant feelings or fatigue. So instead of asking what we feel like eating (that is, what would taste great), we can learn to ask what's the best we can give ourselves, that is, what will make us feel great.

I think this is a secret that healthy people have. They think *That pie looks good but if I eat it, I'll feel sluggish and sleepy and I don't want to feel like that.* I want to think like they do, not like I have in the past: *Wow, that will taste great and I wonder if I can get two pieces and then take the rest home.*

What if being happy, being at peace, and feeling good about ourselves was the lens through which we viewed the world, the lens that dictated our response to opportunities?

FOOD FOR THOUGHT

58 If you've kept journals in the past, what do they reveal about your relationship with food addiction?

59 Which of your stories do you already know need changing?

60 What strengths have your wounding experiences developed in you?

61 What lens now dictates your responses to opportunities?

WE COMMIT TO GROWING UP

62
IN RECOVERY, WE CHOOSE TO GROW UP

In order to recover from addiction, we have to grow up. We have to be adults, in an adult relationship with our body, our emotions, our spirit. We have to take real responsibility for ourselves and care about ourselves in healthier ways.

We have to stop trying to do this alone, and we have to involve others in our healing. We have to keep the lines of communication open, between us and trusted friends, and perhaps a recovery community, and between us and Spirit. It means not isolating, not keeping our cravings a secret or our caving in to them a secret. It means living our lives out in the open, eating out in the open, not acting out in rebellion, not hiding in shame.

I feel considerably more shame about being fat than I've been willing to admit. And it's a very public shame that is reinforced by our culture of self-control. It's sadly far easier to be anorexic or bulimic around food than fat. I know enough about addiction to know that self-control alone doesn't work, but I've been a failure at it where sugar is concerned and that failure is written all over my body as well as on the scale when I'm compulsively overeating.

Growing up means accepting that I'm not going to get thin and get free of addiction without effort. It's accepting that the free ride for my body is over, like needing to stretch before I get out of bed and then stretch even more before I can put my pants on. My body will no longer burn excess calories with any ease; in fact, all the stored sugar contributes to my sore joints and muscles as inflammation. And the extra pounds do too. It's a vicious cycle that I can no longer ignore.

63
GROWING UP AND DEALING WITH NEGATIVE EMOTIONS

Successful recovery from addiction depends on our willingness to grow up. If you're middle-aged or older and reading this, that may sound strange. But most of us started compulsively eating when we were young and in a very real sense, as I said earlier, our emotional development got arrested at the point where we turned our emotional life over to food.

Now that we're taking back the power of our emotions to use for our benefit, not for our destruction, we may have to go through a few tantrums, a few melancholy periods to get there. This can be especially true if you are uncovering your old stories and working on changing them. It can be particularly important for you to have someone supporting your through the process, whether that's a professional listener, a trusted friend, or a recovery group.

People often say that early recovery feels like a second adolescence with its emotional turmoil. In a sense, that's true. Our bodies change in many ways when we start to heal physically from sugar and flour and processed foods. There's a period of detox when the poisons of those products leave our body. We often feel yucky for a couple of weeks or a month and sometimes longer depending on how much toxic crap has been stored in our fat. And as our brains heal, we can feel elated one moment and down in the dumps the next. We have to have the courage and patience to ride through these ups and downs. They will level out.

As addicts, we have a very limited repertoire of ways to handle emotional upset. In fact, most of us had just one way: eat. When we give up that possibility, we can feel at a loss. How do I now deal with my boss, my spouse, my kids? With love, with patience, with self-compassion. We give ourselves and others a break. We lower our expectations. We walk away and breathe. We learn and grow. And we talk about these challenges with our buddies, our small group of fellow addicts if we have one, our 12-Step community, our counselor.

And we have faith that we can do this. We step off the ledge into recovery and somehow the safety net shows up.

64
RECOVERY MEANS TAKING RESPONSIBILITY FOR OUR LIVES—AND OUR BODIES

When we step into recovery from addiction, no matter how reluctant we are, we have to begin to take responsibility for what goes on our plates and in our mouths and into our bodies. We have to take responsibility for our fat as well as for our health. Perhaps even more importantly, we have to take responsibility for our feelings.

For me, responsibility is a double-edged sword. I am not irresponsible in most aspects of my life. My clients can count on me for a job well done and on time. I show up to my appointments early. I pay my bills. I remember birthdays and send cards and gifts. I remember what's important to the people I care about. In fact, I'm so responsible that it can make me want to binge. That's right. For a long time, I've used compulsive eating as a way to be irresponsible.

When we grow up in families that are unsafe or seem that way, some of us become hyper-vigilant and take on responsibility for everyone else. As I said earlier, I am one of those. I concluded that my parents weren't paying much attention—certainly not to me and probably not to anything that could harm us. I got obsessive about everything, worried about everything. Somebody had to, I figured, and it looked like I was the only one.

As a kid, eating four or five candy bars was a way to let down my guard, set down the burden of self-imposed responsibility, and relax a bit. I could reach a point where I didn't care what was going on. This began a terrible pattern in my life, where I had to eat (or drink) to relax. Effort, vigilance, effort, vigilance, effort, vigilance, exhaustion/sugar, rest. Put another way: responsibility, responsibility, responsibility, responsibility, responsibility, burdened/fed-up, irresponsibility (aka sugar).

65
ACCEPTING THE RIGHT KIND OF RESPONSIBILITY

Recovery asks some of us to let go of being responsible for things that aren't ours and instead to create a new relationship with responsibility. It requires us to ask if this issue, this problem is ours to solve. If it is not, recovery means finding new ways to ease up from taking on others' issues, from over-responsibility. For others of us, recovery asks us to take on new responsibilities as mature adults. Living into this new behavior is what 12-Step programs call a *living amend*. A living amend is a change in behavior, often radical, that moves us in the right direction in relationship to ourselves and others.

One of my living amends is to find ways to deal with sugar cravings, to sit with them, feel them, do nothing, and let them pass. I can also try other ways to relax, to put down the burden of responsibility and the weight of anxiety, and I can keep trying until I find ones that are successful.

I can also stop buying treats and I can say no when they are offered. That may seem like a no-brainer, but remember that we are dealing here with addiction, with irrational impulses that reside more in the feeling body than they do in the mental body. Very strong defense mechanisms are invested in my continuing to eat sugar, to soothe myself in that way because it works. So I have to move to some other place in myself, some wiser, more spiritual place in myself where I can honor my body and treat it well. I also have to learn to acknowledge that I am in craving and ride it out.

FOOD FOR THOUGHT

62 What will you have to accept in order to grow up?

63 What safety net could you begin to develop for your recovery?

64 How does responsibility vs. irresponsibility show up in your relationship with food?

65 Where do you need to let go of responsibility and where do you need to take on responsibility?

WE COMMIT TO CHANGING OUR BRAINS

66
WHAT TRIGGERS US

In his wonderful novel, *Animals*, Christian Kiefer's main character is a gambling addict. One of the triggers of his addiction is cash in his pocket. His craving to gamble, his irrational belief that this time it will be different, are stimulated by the feel of the bills in his pocket, which represent the possibility of relief. Each of us addicts has our own triggers, the stimulus from the environment that will start up the cravings. After a while of course, we don't need the triggers. The cravings are constant unless we have just acted on them. I don't have cravings when my belly is full of ice cream. Not for a short while anyway. Then they start up again.

Once we stop using food to soothe ourselves, once we commit to recovery, we have to acknowledge our triggers and eliminate them or at least neutralize them if we are to be successful.

Some of my food addiction triggers are obvious. I get triggered by smells: baking bread, hot chocolate, hot cinnamon. I get triggered by sights: a dessert tray in a fancy restaurant, a picture of an ice cream sundae or milkshake on a picture menu, a waiter going by with a dessert on a plate for another customer. And food addicts aren't the only ones who are triggered this way. This is such a common human response that advertisers count on it. They run those ads for burgers and fries after 10 and not before because after 10, people are getting hungry again and the image will spur them to hit a fast food place.

We recovering food addicts understand the power of visual and smell triggers. We stay out of bakeries, pizza parlors, ice cream shops. We keep our home environment clean of trigger foods. I find eating "family style" with bowls of food on the table is very hard for me. I'm better off to fix my food and put everything out of sight.

67
CRAVINGS: HOW THEY WORK AND HOW TO MANAGE THEM

In doing my research, I came across this interesting discussion of the phenomenon of cravings by Doug Lisle, PhD, a researcher on food addiction. This explained a lot to me.

"Our cravings live and work within a web of images. The targets and goals that drive us are often visual images in our minds. When we think about eating a piece of candy, we actually see an image of it in our minds and then imagine the taste. If you watch your mind work, you will observe that visual images are generally driving the show. You 'see' options for your next move and if you then imagine how it will feel to reach the goal (chomp on the candy), it starts pulling you toward doing it.

"So what is the best technique for managing these types of cravings? The very best technique is basically to not have the cravings in the first place. How is that possible? It is possible when your mind can't create a good image of what the stimulus is going to feel like because it's been a long time since you have actually been exposed to it. The longer the amount of time since you had, say, your last hamburger or fudge sundae, the harder it becomes for your mind to create a vivid image of eating these unhealthy foods. Images depend on memory and memories fade with time. An alcoholic sober for one week has a significantly more difficult problem to manage than an alcoholic sober for a year. Over time, the vividness of memory fades and loses a lot of its destructive influence.

"This is why healthy living can get easier and easier, the better the job you do at it. When you are struggling, you can begin to notice that your cheats tend to come in little streaks. If you have a cheat on Monday, then for the next several days the image of that cheat is forceful since it is very clear in your memory. But if you don't indulge that cheat again for a couple of weeks, the images start to decay in your memory and lose a lot of their power. It can be hard to start a good streak, but it's well worth it. The people who have the best willpower hardly use that willpower at all, since they have rid themselves of their cheats.

"Keep this in mind the next time you are thinking about skipping a treat and staying clean because you don't just win at that moment. You also make tomorrow easier to live healthy and well."

68
CRAVINGS AND PLAYING OUT THE TAPE

In my experience, cravings for the old substances can come without warning. They come without much of a trigger. It's as if some old door in my brain or body or both opens up, and I'm flooded with a very strong need to have a drink or eat a candy bar or go down the ice cream aisle at the grocery store.

Cravings for a drink happened to me a lot when I first got sober but all these years later, they only come once in a great while. When I first let go of sugar and flour, the cravings were quite strong for several weeks and then they began to fade. Now they happen rarely. But when they do, it's unpleasant. I'll be going along in my day, just doing whatever I'm doing, and I'm gripped by a visceral need to eat one of my old demon foods—or all of them. Instead of panicking, I've learned to do what I call *playing out the tape*.

I imagine getting in my car, going to the store, buying the ice cream, coming home. I imagine putting some in a bowl and eating it. I suspect I would enjoy it. Then I remember all the times I put more in the bowl and ate that. And then more in the bowl and ate that. And then I would go back to the store and get a lot more and eat that. And the next day I would do the same thing. And I would be hooked again and in a couple of months I would have regained the weight and the shame and the guilt and fear for my health and the self-loathing, and all my misery would have come back. When I play out this tape, imagine it all to the miserable end of being fully active in my addiction again, my determination to stay in recovery comes to the fore and I can let the desire go.

Playing out the tape takes only a few seconds if you practice it, and I find it so helpful.

69
OTHER KINDS OF TRIGGERS

Less easy to recognize are deeper behavioral triggers. I've noticed that my craving for food or treats is stronger on a Friday afternoon than any other time of the week, especially if I've spent the earlier part of the day with friends in my writing circle. Once everyone leaves, I feel let down and lonely, and I don't want to feel that. In the past, I would have eaten whatever I wanted, even if I had to go to the grocery store and load up, for of course, I wouldn't just get one something. I know now that this is a trigger, so it's a good time for me to go to the bank or take a walk.

In addition, as Lisle says above, the longer we can go without responding to the trigger, the easier that becomes. The more frequently we do that—not respond to the trigger in the old way—the stronger we can make that new brain groove.

Loneliness is thus an emotional trigger for me. For others, it can be anger or a shaming experience. It's important that we learn to recognize what triggers our cravings so that we can pause and figure out a non-food way to care for ourselves.

As I move deeper into recovery, I'm observing other triggers in myself. When I come home from being out, whether to an appointment, a date for lunch, the gym, I want to eat even if it isn't meal time. I call this *transition hunger*. I can see now that I used to have a snack nearly every time I came back home. I suspect that as I stay in recovery, more will be revealed.

FOOD FOR THOUGHT

66 What are some of your food triggers and how can you neutralize them?

67 What do cravings feel like to you?

69 What situations trigger your need to eat compulsively?

TOOLS FOR CHANGE

68 Can you create an inner tape of a particularly negative experience with food that you can play to help yourself ride out a craving?

70
MY OLD BRAIN GROOVE

The idea of addiction as a habit, as a well-worn neural pathway in my brain makes sense to me. I've always assumed that repeated activities, such as driving a car, function like that. When we are learning to drive, we have to pay conscious attention to everything we are doing. But as we become proficient drivers, a good deal of it becomes second nature. We learn to put in the clutch to shift when we need to slow down or speed up without even thinking about it. We learn to look over our shoulder automatically before changing lanes. We put on our seat belts without a conscious thought.

Addiction works in a similar unconscious way. I may pay attention to serving up the first bowl of ice cream because I'm really looking forward to the relief. But as I scoop out each additional bowl in that same evening, I don't notice it. Not the scooping, not the eating. Only when the half-gallon is about gone do I see what I've done.

This ability is really helpful in many ways. We can do lots of helpful things without having to pay attention. Zipping our pants. Turning off the stove. Locking the door. Brushing our teeth before bed. These became automatic.

But with addictive behaviors, this automatic doing isn't helpful. In fact, it contributes to the problem. We speak of this as *mindless* eating but it isn't really. Our brain is engaged in our activity, just not in a completely conscious way. What isn't involved is our conscious Self. When we encounter environmental or emotional triggers that we have responded to with food for so long that the response is automatic, it feels *natural and easy* to respond in that way and *unnatural and hard* to respond in any other way, such as abstinence. This, I believe, is a huge piece of why so many of us food addicts can't stay in recovery for the long haul. Finding ways to be conscious about food with each meal, each trigger is our big challenge.

71
CREATING A NEW BRAIN GROOVE

So, at the heart of successful recovery is the creation of the new pathways in the brain. It is also sometimes referred to as *brain plasticity*, meaning the brain is flexible enough to create new ways of doing things. This flexibility allows us to develop different responses to our old triggers, to do things differently. This is the best possible news for those of us wanting to recover from addiction.

Full-blown addiction doesn't happen overnight. It creeps up on us. We think we are in control of how much we are eating, we think we have choices, and then we are out of control and all choice seems gone. Getting back our power of choice is crucial to recovery.

If we don't exercise choice in each moment, we step back into automatic eating, right back into addiction. Unfortunately, those old brain pathways don't die. They just go dormant as we are establishing the new patterns of behavior. That's why it's so difficult for people who step in and out of recovery. They don't give the new pathways enough of a chance to become automatic; instead, they keep the old patterns alive. This sets up an intensity of craving that can become unbearable.

72
TAKING ADVANTAGE OF OUR BRAIN'S ABILITY TO CHANGE

To create the new brain groove, we have to stay alert, stay conscious, and keep choosing the new way. As Tammy White, a wise teacher of mine, says, "Practice makes permanent. And we are always practicing something." For those of us in recovery, we practice recovery. We practice saying no to the old way of responding and we practice saying yes to the new way.

Here are some of the things I am practicing to create a new brain groove around eating and food.

- I practice maintaining a safe food environment, one that is free of trigger foods.
- I practice writing out my food plan the night before and sending it to my buddy.
- I practice eating what's on my food plan in the specified, weighed amounts.
- I practice planning what I'll eat at a restaurant so I don't need to look at the menu when I get there and be tempted by other ideas.
- I practice being in charge of my food. I practice saying no to pressure from others to eat things that don't work for me. There's a great deal of life we can't control. What we put in our mouths doesn't have to fall into that category. To say it another way, I can be the master of what goes in my mouth, not the victim.
- I practice processing my feelings so they move on and out. I don't fear them and I don't wallow in them. As I heard once at a meeting, feelings are like children in a car: they shouldn't be driving and they shouldn't be stuffed in the trunk.
- I practice talking about my feelings with one or two trusted friends. I don't keep my feelings a secret anymore.

FOOD FOR THOUGHT

70 What are some of the automatic experiences you've had with food and with triggers?

71 What have been your experiences with stepping in and out of recovery?

72 How can you use your brain's ability to create new patterns of behavior to your advantage?

73
PERHAPS THE MOST IMPORTANT THING TO PRACTICE

Active choice, I believe, is the only thing that is going to help me establish those new pathways. This is where my long experience with vigilance can be put to good use. I can watch for triggering situations and avoid them or be aware during them that I have another priority: recovery from food addiction.

I can practice choosing carefully. It's one thing to know intellectually that we always have a choice: go or not go; say yes or say no or say I'll tell you later; eat or not eat. However, I often *act* as if that's not the case. Much of the time when I'm eating compulsively or choosing unwisely, I'm having to override my choice principle. It can happen quickly and it seems unconscious, but I don't think it is. When I eat sugar, I have decided to buy it and then eat it. I make the choice to do so. That means I can make the choice not to do so.

I like the idea of asking myself much more often about choice. What do I want to choose in this moment? What's my good choice in this moment? It will take practice—a lot of it, but I want to be consciously choosing what I do and how I eat rather than being run by old habits.

74
THE BENEFITS OF MY PRACTICE

    Since accepting that I need to practice my recovery every day and since I made a commitment to do that, I have reaped many benefits. Here are some of them

- I feel better physically: thinner, lighter, leaner, cleaner.
- I no longer suffer from food comas and sugar hangovers.
- I have much more stamina.
- I am in a good mood most of the time. I'm consistently happy at 8 or 9 on a 10-point scale. When I'm using sugar, I'm at 4 most days.
- I have much less hip and back pain.
- I can sit in any seat I want.
- I don't need an airplane seatbelt extender anymore.
- Hygiene is easier.
- Walking is easy; stairs aren't daunting anymore.
- I stand up straighter, and I carry myself differently.
- My self-loathing has disappeared.
- My worries about self-destruction have quieted.

75
THE ROLE OF HABITS IN FOOD ADDICTION

When we talk about the old brain groove that needs to go into disuse, we are talking about habits that need to die. There is an habitual part of compulsive eating. But the compulsion to eat itself isn't the habit. It's our response to the compulsion that becomes the habit and that creates the groove in the brain. Here are what some of my addictive food responses (aka *habits*) have looked like:

- Rewarding myself with food treats when I'm working on paid projects that aren't very interesting (my habit response to boredom).
- Stocking up on food treats when I have a long empty weekend ahead (my habit response to anticipated loneliness).
- Eating whenever I think I might be hungry (my habit response to any kind of hunger signals, whether physical or mental or emotional).
- Eating while I watch TV in the evenings (my habit response to restlessness).
- Continuing to eat while I sit at the table with others who eat more slowly than I do (another habit response to restlessness). This is also a habit response to having food visually in my environment (on the table).

Behind each habit, you'll see a feeling that I associate with those behaviors but to be honest, I can't tell you how often I actually feel that emotion when I do the behavior. Because that's the thing about habits. They become automatic responses and actions, like brushing our teeth every night before bed or putting on the brake when we come to a stop sign. We don't think about the behavior. We don't make a conscious decision or choice in response to an idea or a feeling. We just do it.

Like most of our unhealthy habits, overeating serves us. As I've said, medicating with sugar started out as the only way I could find to take care of myself in a childhood that was fraught with fear and anxiety and sadness. It helped me not be with those feelings, which I felt would overwhelm me, maybe even kill me. It was a survival technique. I'm not alone in the childhood origin of my need for soothing. Many of us were too young to deal with those feelings in any other way, and when we got old enough to do something different, we already had the ingrained habit of responding with food.

But we can change habits. We all know we can. We can add behaviors (meditation or balancing our checkbook each month) and delete others (staying up too late or drinking caffeine too late in the day). Of course, compulsive overeating and sugar addiction are much more than a simple habit, but there is a part that is habit, and that part can change. Abstinence and no snacks, which are important parts of my food plan, have become my habit. A healthy food plan can become your habit as well.

FOOD FOR THOUGHT

73 How much choice do you have about food when you are in active addiction? How would choice be an important part of your recovery?

74 What benefits would you like to have from recovery?

75 What habits do you already have that can serve your recovery and what habits need to go? What new habits do you need to develop?

Just start your new practice now, with the next meal, with the next impulse to eat.

—Leo Babauta

76
SOME GOOD SUGGESTIONS FOR BUILDING BETTER HABITS

There are lots of good suggestions out there for creating new habits. Some of the kindest and gentlest come from Leo Babauta in his *Zen Habits* blog. Here is my interpretation of a couple of his ideas.

The first idea, *just start now*, makes me think of an issue I come across often in documents that I edit for clients. The writer will use "tried to" incorrectly to mean a successful effort. *He tried to hug her. She tried to phone him.* And in each of these cases the character succeeded. But that's not what "tried to" means. It means just the opposite. *I tried to call you but you weren't home. I tried to see you but the door was locked.* Effort happens but success does not.

Recently, after I'd been bingeing on caramels for about two weeks, I started trying to stop. Mostly I thought about stopping. I thought about not buying any more. I'd make a plan to not buy any more. And then I'd buy some more and eat them all. I was trying, I really was. The problem was that I was not doing, I was just trying.

Trying to be in recovery doesn't work. Being in recovery does. Trying to eat on your chosen food plan doesn't change much. Eating on your chosen food plan changes a lot. What happens if we stop trying to be abstinent and really be abstinent, however we define that?

77
CHANGE TAKES TIME

Leo Babauta reminds us that change takes time. Acknowledging this time component is critical to recovery. Habits change slowly, and my guess is that the more complicated the habit, the slower the change. That's not such good news for those of us who want relief yesterday! It took me about a year to stop thinking about alcohol every day. In the beginning, I thought about it every few minutes. Grieving its loss was a slow process. But bit by bit, its power over me faded and I thought about it less and less. I seldom think about it now, but I've been in recovery many years.

Building new pathways in the brain takes time. We have to go down that new path continually, use that response over and over and over to make it strong. After 27 years, I have lost my need to respond with alcohol to whatever happens in my life. It no longer even occurs to me to do that. And I also know that the old pathway is still there in my brain. It hasn't gone anywhere and it would not take much to reactivate it.

There are all kinds of theories about how long it takes to create a new habit: 21 days, a month, 6 weeks. For those things that we've been doing most of our lives, I'd say it takes a whole lot longer than that. Although the original course of my food program was an 8-week boot camp, I knew that was just the beginning. Accepting that it will take the rest of my life to recover keeps me out of expecting a quick fix.

78
READJUST IF YOU RETURN TO THE OLD BEHAVIOR. FACE IT, ADMIT IT, START AGAIN.

This idea is very important. When we break our recovery commitment, when we eat a trigger food, when we eat more than is good for us, we can't let that be the end of our food sobriety. We can't afford to fell into resignation. We can't give up. We can't just let the old pathway take over again. Madness and misery lie in that direction. Most of us have been on that merry-go-round a few times already and we know it goes nowhere good.

Leo Babauta talks about *mastering starting*. We can practice making fresh starts in all aspects of our lives. We can see each day, each meal as a fresh start in our recovery. This is a bit of a different spin on the Buddhist idea of *beginner's mind*. We can see each meal as a separate commitment to recovery. We can do that as well each time we ride out a craving without eating something.

If we do relapse, if we slip away from our intention, we can begin again. We must master not only starting, but starting again. In Bright Line Eating, Susan Peirce Thompson calls this "resuming." Perseverance is a key piece in changing our brains and so is resuming.

FOOD FOR THOUGHT

76 Where is *trying* not getting you what you want? Where would *doing* get you?

77 How much time seems realistic to you for changing your food habits?

78 What benefit can you see in making each meal a fresh start?

WE COMMIT TO MANAGING OUR STRESSES

79
THE LIFE THAT SUPPORTS OUR ACTIVE ADDICTION MAY NOT SUPPORT OUR RECOVERY

As I've noted already, most of us addicts create a life that supports our active addiction. We may do so unconsciously but we do it. We live alone so no one comments on our consumption, or we live with others who turn a blind eye to what we are doing or who have their own compulsions that they don't want brought into the light. We stop socializing when it interferes with our consumption, preferring to stay home where we can consume as much as we want. We only shop at stores that carry our favorites, often going out of our way to get there.

Even more importantly, we end up living in a web, a pattern if you will, of stresses that helps us justify our using. Maybe our job is stressful. Maybe our family life is stressful. Maybe we are too lonely, too busy, too overwhelmed. The list is quite individual, but these stresses keep the need for soothing strong. So we go on soothing ourselves in the same old ways with food or drink or drugs or activities to "let off steam."

When we add the stresses of living to our well-ingrained emotional responses of fear and anxiety and depression and worry, our lives are difficult and sometimes unbearable, so we keep on using food to relieve the pain. Abstinence and full recovery cannot thrive in that pressure cooker of difficulty. We may be able to hang on in recovery for a while, "white-knuckling it," as we say in the 12 Steps, but sooner or later, it becomes too much for us and we turn to the old familiar relief.

In order to stay abstinent, to stay fully in recovery, we have to address those stressors and make changes that go beyond just putting down the food.

80
STRESS AND RECOVERY FROM FOOD ADDICTION

It's very difficult to have long-term recovery from food addiction unless we come into a different relationship with our stresses. Although we tend to consider stress negative and avoidable, it is neither. Stress is an inevitable part of life. Some of it is actually good: the anticipation of a vacation, a holiday, a date with a friend or partner. The excitement of a new job or a win for our favorite team. We often don't think of those positive experiences as stresses, but anything that moves us out of a state of calm and equilibrium are stresses.

Most of us are more familiar with negative stresses: difficulties with work, money, health, relationships. And many of us eat over those stresses. Bad day at work? Pizza. Bounced a check? Cheese and crackers. High cholesterol reading? Cookies. An argument with our spouse? Ice cream.

So no matter how successful our food plan, if we don't change how we deal with stress, we will find it very difficult to abstain from our demon foods. Again, how we respond to a stress is a choice and a habit, like most of our behaviors. If we want a different outcome, we have to create new responses to those stresses.

In some ways, this may be the real key to recovery. If we can find the inner strength and external support to be unwavering in our commitment to recovery, to remember that eating is not going to solve the problem that provoked the stress, to remember that eating only adds to the stress, we can find other ways of responding that have a chance to be far more successful in the long run.

81
STRESS AND THE WILLPOWER GAP

We live in a buck-up culture. Vulnerability is not a highly prized trait for us. Thanks again to the Puritans, we don't trust our bodies and we don't trust our feelings. What we do value is discipline, hard work, and willpower. Not rich? You're not working hard enough; you don't have enough discipline. Fat? Where's your discipline? Where's your will power? Buck up.

While the exact nature of willpower is a bit controversial, it's more commonly accepted now that we do not have an infinite supply in any one day. Depending on the amount of stress we subject ourselves to, it can run pretty thin by the end of the day. This explains why parents have more patience with the shenanigans of their children when they're on vacation. Less stress, more ease in responding. If we are stressed all day at work, our diet will fall apart when we come home and need instant soothing. We're good about not snacking all day at work but then we come home and eat a full meal of cheese and crackers before dinner.

This *willpower gap*, as it's called, is a problem for those of us in recovery. We have to ensure we have enough willpower to stay in recovery. That means that we have to build a life between meals that has less stress than other people may be able to tolerate. Consciously reducing our stresses is a skill we must develop if we want to maintain recovery from food addiction.

The 12-Step programs have long known that willpower alone won't keep us abstinent from our drug of choice, in our case, trigger foods. We have to reduce the drama, the difficulties, the stresses so that we can be at peace.

FOOD FOR THOUGHT

79 How does your current life support your active food addiction?

80 How do the current stresses in your life impact your eating?

81 What experiences have you had where willpower was not enough to keep you from compulsive eating?

82
CHANGING HOW WE DEAL WITH STRESS IN OUR WORK

Work is a common stressor for many of us. Why? Because we usually have to deal with a lot of different people: co-workers, bosses, customers. And when humans interact regularly, there's stress. We have differences of opinion. We have different habits and beliefs. We have varying ways of responding. And we have to get along. It can take all of our patience and goodwill to spend eight or more hours a day working with others. When we come home, we no longer have it in us to fix a healthy meal.

Some of us have boring, repetitive jobs. That's a different kind of stress. We look to food to entertain us. The candy stash in the desk drawer. The frequent trips to the break room for more coffee and whatever treats are on the counter. All that sugar and flour spike our dopamine and then we crash and need some more. When we get home, we aren't the least bit interested in a healthy meal.

At the same time, our bodies desperately need good fuel, healthy fuel to soothe our nerves and keep us sane. As food addicts, our mental and emotional health depends, in part, upon eating right. What's more, our recovery depends on that too. So how do we alleviate work stress?

- We feed ourselves well every meal. We make time for a good breakfast with protein and we pack a healthy lunch or dinner, depending on our schedule. We eat well to be calm and clear.
- We do what we can to get demon foods out of our immediate work environment. We go outside at breaks rather than to the break room. We get coffee and move out of the doughnut/cake space. We ask coworkers to support us by keeping things out of sight. We bring fruit and vegetables to the break room.
- We work on our communication skills. We listen more and talk less. If a work policy seems unfair, we speak to our boss or HR. We lower our expectations of others and we raise our expectations of ourselves.

- We educate ourselves. We take courses in nonviolent communication or personal transformation. We can't change others but we can change ourselves. That's what recovery from addiction is all about, creating a life that supports recovery.
- We change jobs or careers if we can. About five years into sobriety, I could see that college teaching wasn't going to work for me anymore. I had been in it 18 years at that point and my friends all thought I was crazy to quit. But I moved west to be nearer my family with only the promise of a job as a receptionist at much less pay. I knew that my recovery depended on less stress and more happiness, and I trusted that I could figure something else out. And I did.
- We make sure that if we are stuck where we are (that no other feasible possibilities truly exist in our circumstances—for example, we live in a small town or poor economy), we do what we can to make our personal work circumstances as good as they can be.

83
DEALING WITH FINANCIAL STRESS

Financial stress and work stress often go hand in hand. Unhappy at work, we eat and spend to entertain and soothe ourselves. Because many addicts are fueled by dissatisfaction, we overspend in a vain attempt to fill the hole. We buy food, treats, toys, clothes—whatever we think will make us feel better. There can seem to be so little difference between a little credit card debt and a lot of credit card debt that we extend our what-the-hell attitude from what we eat to what we spend. At the same time, our overspending can keep us stuck in a job we hate and that fuels our overeating. It's a vicious cycle of the first degree.

When I first got sober, I had a lot of credit card debt from vacations I couldn't afford. A wise and kind financial planner told me to get out of debt as quickly as possible: cut my expenses, do whatever it took. Only then should I start saving money every month to have a cushion. I was a single woman and although he was about my age, I could see the fatherly advice there to figure out ways to really take care of myself. I followed his advice. Focusing on paying off debt and then saving gave me a different relationship with money, which, before that time, had been all about earning and spending. I didn't realize until later that he was helping me develop a practice that would alleviate financial stress in my life.

The 12 Steps encourage those in recovery to practice recovery principles in all their affairs (this is actually Step 12). Money and our worries around it can create enormous difficulties for the calm and peace of mind we need to eat well. Finding ways to relieve financial stress can go a long way to supporting our recovery and a healthy relationship with food.

CANDY GIRL

84
GROUP SUPPORT FOR ALLEVIATING FINANCIAL STRESS

Another huge help for me has been my Women and Money group. About 12 years ago, I realized I needed to alter my relationship with money even further, so I invited friends and friends of friends to join me in doing that together. We still meet once a month on a late Sunday morning. Members have come and met their goals and moved on, but some of us are in it for the long haul.

In the beginning, we read several books together, including Suzie Orman's *Women and Money*, Lynne Twist's *The Soul of Money*, and Vicki Robbins' *Your Money or Your Life*; and we established simple ground rules for our group.

1. The only requirement for membership is that each member has an up-to-date will and an advance medical directive by the end of the first six months of participation. If they don't meet that goal, they are out until they do. They can do this online or with a lawyer. Women very often don't have a will or a medical directive and this is an important first step for putting your financial life in order.
2. We deal with earning, spending, and saving. We don't discuss investments or investment strategies as there's lots of other kinds of support for that piece.
3. Each woman sets her own goals for earning, spending, and saving. One of our members got out of $32,000 of credit card debt in her first three years in the group. Another figured out retirement for herself, quit her job, sold her house in town, and bought a duplex at the beach. Others of us have built up large savings accounts.
4. At each meeting, we review what we accomplished on our commitment list for the month before, we discuss any general topics anybody wants to bring up, and we set modest goals for the next month.

None of us are true spending addicts (if you are, you might want to consider Debtors Anonymous, the corresponding 12-Step group), but we all had and sometimes still have unhealthy relationships with money. Together we are making great strides forwards.

FOOD FOR THOUGHT

82 What work stresses are impacting your food addiction? How might you reduce some of that stress?

83 What financial stresses may be fueling your eating patterns? How might you also get into recovery from overspending?

84 How might a group like the one described in #84 support you in reducing your financial stress?

85
DOING WHAT WE CAN TO ALLEVIATE RELATIONSHIP STRESSES

As noted above, human interactions are frequently stressful. Most of us want things to go smoothly all the time, and that just doesn't happen. Humans disagree with each other. We have emotional baggage, sometimes serious trauma, from childhood or earlier relationships that influence how we respond to others. We may have trouble setting boundaries or easing up on expectations.

Again, we need to learn a variety of coping skills that can help us navigate the inevitable ups and downs without falling back into our compulsive eating habits. Some of us need a spiritual director, counselor, or therapist to help us develop those skills. We may need to set aside any shame we feel in asking for such help in order to support our recovery.

Those of us who live alone have some advantage here. We can usually create a stress-free environment around food by not having demon foods in the house and only inviting in people with whom we have easy and comfortable relationships. But many food addicts live with families that have been created in the dysfunction and chaos of addiction. When we start to change our behaviors and attitudes, those around us can feel threatened and more anxious than ever, especially if they are also addicts of any sort. Your food addict or alcoholic wife or husband may not want to join you in recovery. Your pot-smoking teenager may not be interested in a drug-free home.

These are difficult circumstances to deal with and I have no simple answers to give you. Part of my own recovery was extricating myself from an abusive primary relationship of 10 years. We were both addicts, and when I got sober, he did not want to look at his own addictive behaviors. I knew I wasn't safe there and I had to leave. It was a slow and painful process but after a year, I was on my own and my healing accelerated.

If you live with other addicts, you are living in chaos and that will not support your recovery. If you have serious relationship stresses, please seek help through a counselor or minister or the EAP office at your work place.

86
HEALTH STRESSES

Stress from poor health is inevitable for most of us, whether it be the minor stress of a cold or flu that keeps us from work and makes us miserable or the major stress of a serious illness in ourselves or those we love and care for.

Minor health issues can reactivate old ways of taking care of ourselves. Sometimes this can take the form of feeding ourselves anything we want so we can feel better or get so numb we don't care that we don't feel good. Frozen pizza or toast and jam to tempt our appetite. Ice cream to medicate a sore throat. A gallon of orange juice for vitamin C without thinking about the huge sugar intake that means. We can easily revert to the old soothers when we're ill. It takes something extra to stay abstinent when we don't feel good physically.

Fortunately, when we're eating only healthy foods, we tend to not get sick very often. The large quantities of fruits and vegetables I eat on my food program are wonderful for my immune system. In addition, eating three moderate meals a day means my body is no longer overburdened by the need to constantly be digesting food. (Did you know that a huge part of your immune system lives in your intestines?) But we will get sick and having a strong recovery program makes it easier to resist the temptation to eat demon foods.

Major health issues are different in some ways and not different in others. When we have major health problems, our resolve and commitment can be heavily taxed. We get anxious, fearful, angry, tired, and lonely. We want to soothe those things and our automatic soothing behaviors crowd in to "help" us. If we've built a strong repertoire of non-food soothers, we will be better equipped to choose something else. In addition, when we are solidly in recovery, we take better care of ourselves overall. We tend to exercise, we get medical and dental checkups, we seek help when something goes wrong rather than wishing it away. And we continue to learn how to take care of ourselves emotionally rather than stuffing down unwanted feelings with food.

And we can be kind to ourselves if we do eat off our plan. And we can return as quickly as possible to eating the kinds of healthy foods that will give our body the fuel and healing it seeks. We can also remember that sugar, flour, and processed foods have too few nutrients to be of any help in treating our illness.

87
THE STRESS OF PRETENDING TO BE NORMAL

There's one final stress that only addicts know: the stress of pretending to be normal. When we eat with others, we pretend we are satisfied with a small portion. We pretend we don't want another piece of cake or another serving of ice cream. We volunteer to do the dishes so we can get into the kitchen by ourselves and eat more of whatever great food is still on the counter with no one watching.

When we shop, we pretend we're having a party so the checkout guy won't think all the sweets and chips are just for us. We pretend we're too tired to go out when friends invite us, preferring to stay home and eat all we want without the shame of anyone watching.

Some of us pretend we have metabolic problems to explain our obesity. We pretend diets don't work when we know we couldn't stick to the regimen. We wear baggy clothes and a lot of black so we can pretend no one can see the results of our compulsive eating. We pretend we don't need to go to the doctor because we are afraid she will want us to get on the scale. Worst of all, we pretend we don't care that we are addicts, that we are fat. We get defiant and angry when friends or family express concern.

All of this pretense is a terrible stress on us because it is extremely painful to live so far out of alignment with our best selves, so far off the mark from what we know we should do for ourselves.

When we step into recovery, when we live committed to letting go of our compulsive eating and living a different life, all this pretense is lifted from us. We can begin to be our real selves all the time. It's amazing to shed that pain and that stress.

FOOD FOR THOUGHT

85 What relationship stresses are active in your life? What's one step you could take to resolve that?

86 How does compulsive overeating contribute to any health stresses you are facing?

87 What are some of your experiences of pretending to be a normal eater or of hiding your compulsive eating?

88
WE USUALLY NEED TO GO SLOW AND MAKE INCREMENTAL CHANGES

Much as we may want to change our lives overnight to escape the painful burden of our addiction, we often have to move slowly. Too much change all at once can throw us back into the arms of soothing with food. But that doesn't mean we can't start moving. And one of the best first steps is to identify our stresses and create an action plan to address them.

One way to start easing the stress is to attend to the small things. If your daily commute is a stressor, start leaving 10 minutes earlier. If getting the kids ready for school wears you out, do as much preparation the night before as possible (their clothes and yours laid out, everyone showered at night, lunches and breakfast prepared). Once we sort out the minor stresses and alleviate them, we free up energy to tackle the bigger issues.

There's one exception to moving slowly. If you are in an abusive relationship with a spouse or boss, get out as fast as you can. Find support and just go even if the exit isn't smooth or the alternative plan ideal. Abuse doesn't usually stop until we leave.

89
IDENTIFY YOUR STRESSES

Here's a way to identify your stresses and get a clearer picture of what might need to change. You probably already have a good idea of what some of these things are.

- Over the next 10 days, keep a running list of what uses up your patience. A simple way to do this is to put a 3x5 index card in your purse or pocket and jot things done as they occur. Or you can do this before you go to bed. Create a new list each day and include anything that may have already appeared on earlier lists. You're looking for repetitions and patterns.
- On Day 11, read through your cards. Cross off anything that occurred only once unless it was a huge stressor. Note any patterns you see, any things that keep showing up.
- On a new list or card, transfer the top 10 stressors. Then ask yourself these questions about each one.

1. On a scale of 1-10, how stressed does this make me feel? How likely am I to eat over this to make myself feel better?
2. Is this something I can easily change? What could I do? Am I willing to do it? Do I need support to do it? What would that look like and who could I ask?
3. Would a major life change be required to address this? If so, set that card aside for now.

90
CREATE AN ACTION PLAN FOR ALLEVIATING A MAJOR STRESSOR

Because major stressors impact so much of our lives, creating an action plan is a great next step. While you can write one out on your own, getting help from your counselor, buddy, or coach will be really useful. Here are some ideas.

Start with figuring out what you really want to have. You don't need to know all the particulars but the more you define and refine what will make the most positive change for you, the more effective your action plan may be. Here are some ways to consider phrasing your desire:
- I want more peace in my marriage.
- I want to work from home.
- I want to pay off all my debts.
- I want to enjoy being at work and be excited to go there.
- I want to be asthma-free.

Next, make a list of as many ways as you can think of (don't just be practical) to get what you want. A fun next step is to do the 16 Solutions game on this (see #163).

Once you know the end result you're looking for and have some ideas for getting there, you can begin to create a very loose and detailed action plan. Here are some questions to ask as you start the process.
1. How might I get from where I am to where I want to be?
2. Who might help me with ideas of how to do that?
3. If I make changes, who else will be affected? How can I enroll their participation?
4. How can I stay out of overwhelm?
5. Is there a buddy or a group I could join or create that could support me in doing this?
6. What is a realistic timeframe for this?
7. What are some first steps I could take?

FOOD FOR THOUGHT

88 What small, incremental changes could you make to alleviate one of the stresses in your life? Can you do that today?

89 If you have done the exercise in #89, what did you learn about yourself that will be helpful in your recovery from compulsive eating?

90 What other ideas do you have for managing a stress-reduction project?

TOOLS FOR CHANGE

89 Do the exercise in #89 to identify your stresses. Choose one stress and find ways to begin to reduce it in your life.

90 Create an action plan for each of the desires you identified in #90. Bit by bit, put them into play.

91
CHOOSING PEACE OVER DRAMA

Many of us mistake drama for the meaningful. This error is fostered and perpetuated by the media and not just the news but TV and the movies and the Internet. The dangerous, the scandalous, that seems to be real life, not going to bed early and getting up early and fixing meals for yourself and your family, not going to a job that isn't thrilling but pays your mortgage and dental bills and keeps food in the house.

And most drama is fueled by anger and resentment and fear. These emotions, while natural and inevitable to some extent, are very hard on those of us in recovery. We can handle them in small doses: the occasional disagreement, the once-in-a-while argument, but if we get a steady diet of anger and fear and resentment, we are prone to relapse as our need for soothing will outweigh our commitment to health.

Some of us have attracted lots of drama into our lives by the choices we've made: bad relationships with partners, dodgy financial schemes, accepting abuse from bosses or coworkers. In a way, the associated adrenalin made us feel more alive than peace and contentment. But it also drove us to soothe with food and perhaps other addictive substances and behaviors, like overworking. So if we are going to maintain recovery from addiction, we have to cultivate peace and contentment rather than steady excitement and drama. We can start, as I said earlier, by looking for ways to reduce stress in our lives. And we can trust that life will send us all the drama we need without our asking for more.

92
GET HELP FOR TOUGH DECISIONS

Eliminating our stresses is easy to say and not easy to do. It sounds simple: get a new job or career, leave your addict spouse, set boundaries with your kids or coworkers that facilitate your abstinence. But making these kinds of big changes takes time and a lot of support. So again it's best to move slowly in most circumstances and get help for your tough decisions.

Seek out a professional: If you belong to a church, your pastor or priest may be a good resource, either as someone to talk to or for a referral to a counselor or therapist. If you have health insurance, ask your provider for a list of counselors who have experience with addiction. Crisis hotlines are another good resource for names.

If money for professional help is an issue, consider 12-Step programs. Overeaters Anonymous is a great support for recovery from food issues, especially the HOW or Gray Sheet meetings, which deal with sugar and flour addiction. Alanon is a wonderful program that teaches you how to take care of yourself as you deal with an addict in your life. All 12-Step programs are free and open to anyone with a desire to stop doing addictive behaviors. Members who've been around a while volunteer to sponsor others who need support.

Get a buddy: Look around you. Is there a friend or family member who is also suffering from obesity or food issues? Is there someone at work? While their food program may be different from yours, if you are both committed to change and to supporting each other in eating differently, moving more, and creating happier lives between meals, you can achieve a lot of success together.

Create a leaderless group: Put out word through email or social media that you're looking for others who are struggling with food issues and who would like to offer each other mutual support. If you find enough local folks, you can have in-person meetings or you can meet online via Skype or Google Hangout. A simple format is the 4 Cs: check-in, celebrations, challenges, and commitments.

Work with a life coach: Life coaches are great for sorting out where you want to go now and figuring out how to get there. If you can find one with experience in food addiction, so much the better (see **www.lifebetweenmealscoaching.com** for more ideas).

93
TAKE RESPONSIBILITY FOR YOUR SUCCESS

In the end though, no matter how much help we find, we are the only one who can make the changes we need. We're the only one who can stop putting sugar and flour or excess food into our bodies. We're the only one who can eat on a schedule if that is what works best for us. We can't abdicate responsibility for this to someone else. We can ask for help, we can accept help, but we have to do the work. It's our responsibility.

The same is true of most of the changes that support that recovery. We have to find the courage to speak up for what we need: a sugar-free home environment, less stress at work, financial independence, whatever it takes. The Big Book of AA puts it quite succinctly: "Half-measures availed us nothing." We need to be all in if we want to succeed at being free of food addiction.

FOOD FOR THOUGHT

91 What role has drama played in your addiction (perhaps in your excuses and justifications)? How can you reduce the drama in your life?

92 Whom do you know who could help you with your decision and strategy? Make a list and begin talking to them.

93 What are some things you would need to do to create success in recovery from compulsive eating?

TOOLS FOR CHANGE

92 Enlisting a buddy to work with is invaluable. Take that on this week.

WE COMMIT TO ABSTINENCE IN ONE FORM OR ANOTHER

94
WHAT IS ABSTINENCE?

For food addicts, abstinence means not eating certain things or not eating in certain ways. When we diet, we practice some form of abstinence so the idea isn't unfamiliar to us. The complication comes when we must decide what to be abstinent from. Diets typically tell us what not to eat. But that isn't always helpful, as any particular diet may not ask for abstinence from foods that trigger us individually. In addition, diets are only asking for short-term abstinence, and it's long-term abstinence that supports recovery from food addiction.

Recovery from food addiction is also more complicated than recovery from alcohol and drugs because we can abstain completely from drugs and alcohol but we can't abstain completely from food. We must eat to be healthy.

But while a very small number of food addicts are addicted to the act of eating itself (chewing and swallowing), most of us are much more discriminating. Our compulsive overeating occurs with what I call *demon foods*: sugar, flour, fat, and other processed foods. You probably know them as candy, ice cream, chips, baked goods, desserts, pancakes, muffins, snack bars, popcorn. You get the idea. If we abstain from those foods, we have a good shot at recovery.

Abstaining is not the same as eating in moderation. Abstaining is not eating those foods at all. Ever. In any quantity. Abstaining is removing those foods from our diet now and forever. This is the hard part. But there is good news. Many of us addicts have black-and-white, all-or-nothing thinking and abstinence is a place where we can put that to good use. We can stop consuming what's killing us.

95
I HAD TO SURRENDER TO ABSTINENCE

Abstinence from alcohol is a simple idea. Don't drink alcohol. Period. But abstinence around food is so complicated, Overeaters Anonymous has a 225-page book in which 200+ members describe what abstinence means to them. That's not surprising. A recovering alcoholic can go her whole rest of her life without taking a drink. She can arrange her life so that she never even comes into contact with alcohol. A recovering food addict, however, has to deal with food every day. We have to eat. I found that idea plus my AA experience a terrific combination of excuses to not get abstinent with food.

Abstinence from alcohol, once I surrendered, was not too much of a struggle. I knew that if I didn't stop drinking, I would die, most likely by my own hand. But since I had to eat, how could I be abstinent? I had to eat, didn't I?

It is true that for some compulsive overeaters, there is a life-and-death aspect. These people are typically diabetic and already suffering from the ravages of that disease. The most inspiring person I met in my time in OA was a man with diabetes who had 20 years of continuous abstinence as he defined it. Sticking to his food plan meant life and a real possibility of longevity. Veering from it meant debilitating illness and death.

But for most of us, those consequences seem too far down the road for the threat to be helpful. Our problems are less dire and therefore easier to set aside, if not ignore, things like uncomfortable airplane seats and the humiliation of asking for a seatbelt extender. Choosing a table instead of a booth at a restaurant in order to be comfortable. Achy joints, difficulty with more than one flight of stairs, little interest in lots of physical activity. Feeling stuffed or queasy, digestive systems that don't work so well or that work unpredictably, difficulty putting on our socks. These consequences of overeating and excess weight are annoying and even depressing, but they don't evoke fear, just shame.

I had the shame but I didn't have the fear. And I still didn't want to be a food addict. But I knew that something had to change. And I came to understand that overeating, for me, is a separate but related problem; that at the heart of it is my addiction to sugar and flour. The important piece of this is that I can abstain from sugar and flour. I can also give up how complicated abstinence might look in the abstract and accept that I can abstain from all foods that trigger me. I can also learn to abstain from overeating.

96
MOVING AWAY FROM ABSTINENCE AS PUNISHMENT

If I move up from the foundation of abstinence as a physical plan of eating and not-eating and as a new habit to build, I arrive at abstinence as a support for healthy physical and emotional living instead of a restriction, a punishment for past bad behavior.

When I'm eating compulsively, these appear to be my values and beliefs:
- I need and deserve immediate relief from whatever is bothering me.
- Food works best for this.
- I'll never be free of my painful feelings any other way except by eating right now.
- Immediate pleasure is the only antidote for my pain (restlessness, boredom, loneliness, sadness, you name it).
- I have to take care of myself because no one else cares.

With values like these, it's no wonder that abstinence would seem like punishment to me. I had to release these beliefs for something that served me better.

97
ADOPTING ABSTINENCE AS A HELPFUL ATTITUDE

I am a believer in the idea that our minds create our experiences. And values and attitudes exist only in the mind. So how can my mind create a new experience with food? How do I adopt the attitude, the belief that abstinence from compulsive eating is in my best interest? How do I change my beliefs and values around eating?

Here are the beliefs and values that I am stepping into in recovery from food addiction:

- I am able and willing to have a healthy relationship with food.
- Sugar and flour are poison to my mind and body. (I have plenty of proof of this.)
- Millions of people deal with their feelings and their problems without eating over them. I can do this too.
- Being healthy in mind and body is my #1 priority.
- I can be with my feelings and let them pass through me.

My good friend Sage Cohen spoke recently at a gathering about shifting her eating patterns and choices. "I'm realizing," she said, "that my body is my most important asset and that I need to eat as if my life depends on it." This resonated with me. Abstinence from demon foods is a gift I can make to my body and my general well-being.

98
ABSTINENCE FOR ME INCLUDES NO SNACKS

In Bright Line Eating, the program I follow, the revolution in the food plan was not no sugar or other sweeteners. I knew I was addicted to sugar and had to let it go. It wasn't even no flour of any kind. I understood pretty quickly the chemistry of this. Take healthy grains and pulverize them, and you significantly reduce the nutrition and remove most of the healthy fiber. Then the resulting sugars (yes, sugars because the body responds to flour as a sugar) go right to the brain of the addict just as if it were a candy bar. This was why being gluten-free didn't help me. I just moved to rice flour products, corn meal, potato flour for my bread, pasta, crackers. I was still eating processed carbohydrates or, I should say, I was still compulsively overeating them. It was just like sugar in my system.

No, the real revolution for me was the third Bright Line: no snacks. Three meals a day and no snacks. Here's why it was revolutionary: I had always snacked. I was a chronic snacker. I had all kinds of snack habits. I ate breakfast before the gym and had a snack afterwards. If I was meeting a friend for a late lunch or dinner, I'd have a snack a couple of hours before. I always carried food with me in my purse or the glove compartment of my car. If I bought groceries, I'd have a snack while I put the food away. If I was bored or restless at my desk, I'd get a snack. If I need a break, I'd get a snack.

In the early days of my dieting, the snacks were low-fat but that almost always means high sugar and that just sets me to bingeing. And many of the so-called healthy snacks are full of sugar, even if they are made with dried fruit. These became impossible for me as I couldn't eat them in moderation. And if I tell the truth, most of my life, I have collapsed snack into treat. It's a hard habit to break. I want treats, I deserve treats, I need treats, I'm entitled to treats. Remember our earlier conversation about entitlements?

Now I don't do treats. I eat three meals a day and I abstain from all sugars, all flours, and all snacks. No snacks. It's astounding to me that I have been able to do this. The first few days were very hard. My inner child was screaming at me. I was off sugar, off flour, and off snacks. But as the days went by, it got easier. And I hadn't realized how much I was eating between meals until I stopped.

But the need for it has faded. The habit has faded. I'm building a new neural pathway that doesn't include snacking. Oh, I get hungry between meals. I do. But I don't eat. I just don't.

99
DOES ABSTINENCE MEAN I HAVE TO DO IT PERFECTLY?

The simple answer to this question is yes. Abstinence means we don't eat the foods that harm us. Again we just don't. The dream of moderation has always haunted addicts. *Maybe someday,* we think, *I'll figure out how to eat like a normal person.* But the truth is we won't. Our brains and bodies have been fundamentally altered by our addictive patterns so the best we can hope for is long-term remission. And remission is possible only if we don't consume those substances that are addictive to each of us.

The more complicated answer to the question is that we just don't know. Is a trace of sugar in a salad dressing going to reactivate my cravings for sugar? So far that hasn't been my experience. If sugar is way down the list of ingredients, it doesn't seem to be a problem for me. But I won't eat honey mustard dressing or poppy seed dressing, both high in sugar. Some people decide to play around with foods, to try them and find out. Me, I don't want to do that. Here's why? I don't want a little bit of sugar. I don't want one cookie or one ice cream bar. I want all I want until I'm sick and even then I want more. That's the way addiction plays out for me.

So I keep strictly to my commitment. No sugars, no flours, no snacks. I eat whole foods and plenty of them. I eat well. And I let the rest go. For me, it isn't about perfection. It's about safety and health.

100
WHAT ABOUT RELAPSE?

Relapse is what we call going back into active addiction. Some people survive relapse and make it back to abstinence. Most don't. Addiction is cunning, baffling, and powerful as we say in the 12-Step programs. It does not go away. It just goes quiet when we are in recovery and it can be reactivated in a nanosecond. One doughnut leads to two dozen. One potato chip leads to a bag or two. We all know this. We've been there and done that. "Bet you can't eat just one." You're right. I can't.

The easiest way to deal with relapse is to stay abstinent. Those who have done the research (aka *relapsed*) tell the same story. It wasn't worth it. The food didn't taste all that great and the weight came back on unbelievably fast (remember, your fat cells don't go away either; they're just waiting to be refilled) and they were miserable very quickly. I don't want my misery back.

If you do relapse, get back on track as quick as you can. Call your buddy or someone in your small group and tell them what you've done. Email me. Get rid of the foods. Stop going to that store or restaurant or coffee shop. Start over now. Don't wait for Monday or the first of the month. That's your addiction in action. Get back into recovery on your next meal. You probably won't want to. That's addiction talking too. Remember addiction isn't rational. It isn't logical.

Most importantly, remember what you really want. For me, it's health, freedom, and the happiness of having a right-sized body.

FOOD FOR THOUGHT

94 What forms of abstinence have you practiced in the past?

95 How do you feel emotionally about abstaining from your trigger foods? How does this response stand in your way?

96 What attitudes might you need to shift to fully enter into recovery from compulsive eating? How might you move from viewing abstinence as limitation and punishment to viewing it as helpful?

97 What new beliefs and values would give you a positive relationship with abstinence?

98 What is your relationship with snacking? How does it impact your food addiction?

TOOLS FOR CHANGE

99 Write out the healthiest abstinence plan you can imagine for yourself. Read it every day for two weeks to see if you can accept it as a reality for yourself.

100 Write out what you really want from your recovery. Put a copy in your purse. Put a copy on your fridge. Read it often.

WE COMMIT TO CHANGING OUR LIVES

*I am here today
because my commitment to living my potential is greater
than my commitment to the familiar.*

—Gay Hendricks, life coach and author

101
MOVING OUT OF STUCK INTO SATISFACTION

One thing most addicts share is a well-worn experience with being stuck. That adage about insanity occurring when we do the same things over and over and expect different results? It's true, and nowhere is it more true than in active addiction.

We overeat and hope we won't feel terrible, hope we won't gain weight this time. But of course we do. Instead of giving up that false expectation, we hang in there and get stuck in that pattern. We try diets and aren't successful but we keep looking for the magic two-week solution or the pill that will make our fat melt away. That's another pattern we get stuck in. Or we get stuck in denial that there is a solution. *I'll always be fat,* we tell ourselves, *I might as well be more fat.*

The truth is that there are a fair number of ways to lose the weight and it's pretty basic. Eat less than you need to maintain your weight. Do this consistently and steadily and eventually most of our bodies will respond, if we have the patience and commitment to keep at it. We know this.

But to move out of the pattern of losing and gaining it all back and then some, we have to create a different life. We have to build a life of such satisfaction that being stuck in overeating and addiction isn't an option anymore. We have to change more of our patterns than just how and what and how much we eat. We have to create circumstances that support our recovery.

102
THE NEED FOR A STRUCTURED LIFE

I don't remember a lot from my first days at the alcohol treatment center. They had given me drugs to alleviate the worst of the withdrawal from alcohol poisoning. But I do remember the Monday morning lecture of my first week about creating a structured life to support my recovery.

"Addiction loves chaos," said the counselor. "Erratic bedtimes, erratic meals or no meals, snacking at all hours, using at all hours. Not showering on the weekends. Your addiction loves this. But it won't support your recovery. Here you'll go to bed at the same time and get up at the same time every day. We want you to do this when you get home. Eat your meals on a schedule. Go to work and be on time. Take your breaks on time. Keep chaos out of your life."

I took this to heart, and structure supported my recovery from alcohol and it now supports my recovery from food addiction. I go to bed and get up at roughly the same time every day. It's not rigid, not to the minute. But I've trained my body to get sleepy as 9:30 rolls around and to wake up when it gets light. My day goes better this way. I'm calmer, more at peace.

I also eat my meals on a schedule of my choosing. Again, it isn't rigid and my days aren't always the same. I am committed to going four to five hours between meals, so each morning I sort out my day and plan when those meals will be. I'm flexible; for example, a 1 pm lunch can become a 1:30 lunch if need be. But it's a schedule and I believe my recovery and abstinence are stronger for it.

103
WHY WE HAVE TO CHANGE HOW WE EAT AS WELL AS WHAT WE EAT

Being thin has never made me happier. I was thin as a child, as a teenager, and as a young woman, and I was not happy. Many people have this same experience. They lose the weight but they're not happier. Why? Because their life doesn't change when their body does. They still have the same circumstances and the same issues. They carry the same emotional baggage; they live in the same stresses and disappointments.

This is one of the big reasons long-term recovery rates are so low (about 10% of those who enter recovery stay in recovery). People put down the ice cream and the chips, but the same stresses they were trying to escape through active addiction are still there. They're still anxious, unhappy, angry, bored, restless, and discontent, but now they have no anesthetic to smooth over those feelings. And while we can find the courage to be uncomfortable until things pass, serious stressors that are chronically or repeatedly there are just too much to handle and we go back to the anesthetic.

To stay in recovery, we need to change our lives, sometimes a little, sometimes a lot. We need to reduce and eliminate the stressors. We also will be better off if we find new ways to soothe and satisfy ourselves. We need to find ways to create a life of happiness and satisfaction and meaning so that the old addicted way of living loses its appeal.

104
BUILDING A 3-MEAL LIFE

Before I found Bright Line eating, I hadn't had a 3-meal life since I learned to feed myself as a child. As I said earlier, snacking has been akin to breathing for me. As a skinny child, I was hungry all the time, as a growing adolescent, even more so. I began developing my addiction to sugar and flour about fourth grade when I would come home from school and eat 4 or 5 pieces of buttered toast with jam or cinnamon and sugar. And as I said earlier, I ate candy during the day at school. In college, my dorm room was full of sweet snacks, hidden of course from my roommate.

I always had snacks with me. Nuts, candy, cheese, half a sandwich. I needed it to be safe, I guess. I've always eaten at work, in the library in college, in the car. In some of the worst of my addiction, I ate during the night, getting up for bowls of ice cream to tide me over until breakfast.

I used to pride myself on being a most flexible meal companion. Need to eat dinner early? No problem. I can snack later. Need to eat late? I can snack before. I fully embraced six small meals a day as license to graze, although that wasn't really what I was doing. I was eating all day long.

Now I eat three meals a day. Period. And while I like my structure, recently at a conference, I went 7 hours between lunch and dinner. I didn't faint, I didn't die. I had been told I'd get hungry but that the hunger would pass. It did. I more than survived. I was totally okay. I also am learning to ask for what I need for this 3-meal life. If I'm eating with others, I negotiate meal times when possible so I don't have to eat too early or too late.

I do make one exception to the 3-meal life: the days I go to the gym early in the morning. I've discovered that I can't go on an empty stomach and I can't go on a full stomach. So I split my breakfast on those days, eating half before the gym and the other half right after.

105
MORE ON HOW I'VE CHANGED MY FOOD LIFE

Here are some of the ways I have changed my food life to support my recovery.
- I eat on a schedule. Each day I figure out what my lunch plans are (it's the most movable meal of the day). I eat breakfast five hours before my lunch meal and I eat dinner five hours after. I can eat dinner later than that but I don't usually because I'm hungry when it comes time to eat!
- At home, I weigh and measure my portions. When I eat out, I use the one plate rule with more vegetables than protein.
- If I eat out, I choose from the menu online before I go to the restaurant.
- I keep my bedtime steady at 10 pm with only an occasional exception for a theater night. I am always up by 7 am, often earlier, depending on the season. My body naturally wakes up with the light.
- I grocery shop on Wednesdays (senior discount day) and stay out of food stores the rest of the week. If I don't have something, I make do with what I have.
- I keep a small but well-stocked pantry of foods that are on my plan. This includes a few canned items (organic chili, beans, some vegetables) and frozen vegetables and fruit and meat.
- I cook once a week, so that I have plenty of food ready to eat when meal time comes. When it's time to eat, I don't want to wait an hour to have things be ready.
- Each night after dinner, I write down my meals for the next day and I email them to my buddy. I also write in a 5-year journal how my day has been and what my happiness and hunger ratings were. I like keeping track. I also put my weight down in that journal if it has been a scale day.
- I weigh myself once a week, usually Monday mornings before I get dressed.
- I am making my relationship with food more and more automatic.

FOOD FOR THOUGHT

101 Where are you stuck in your life? Where are you unsatisfied? How can you use that dissatisfaction to begin to make changes in your life to support your recovery?

102 What kind of structures in your day might support your recovery?

103 As you've worked through the questions on the preceding pages, what are you coming to see that needs to change in your life for your recovery to be successful?

104 Would a 3-meal life support your recovery? How could you work that out?

105 Which of my changes might work for you? Which might you modify to better suit your recovery? What else might you add?

TOOLS FOR CHANGE

Create a plan for your recovery. Add details until you're satisfied. Begin implementing parts of it over the next few weeks.

To make life meaningful, you must decide that life matters, that your efforts matter, and that you matter, regardless of any apparent evidence to the contrary.

—Dr. Eric Maisel, *Why Smart People Hurt*

106
HOW CREATING A MEANINGFUL LIFE BETWEEN MEALS SUPPORTS RECOVERY

Most of us associate recovery with abstinence, with what we need to give up. We don't associate it with what we need to take on. In my first years of recovery from alcoholism, no one ever talked to me about the importance of having a meaningful life, not until I read the *Artist's Way* by Julia Cameron. Cameron is a recovering alcoholic who found herself unable to continue her career as a screenwriter since she was no longer fueled by alcohol. She developed a program to regain her creativity and then began sharing it with others. Through her program, I too was able to regain my sense of myself as a creative and even more importantly, I began to see a way to access more meaning in my life.

I think many of us addicts are perplexed and confused by life. We know it holds some important secret, some deeper meaning than the everyday events we live through, but unless we find that meaning in religion, we experience a fruitless search. Education doesn't seem to bring it to us. Neither does sex and romance although they may do so briefly.

For some reason, we feel better when we are in high drama, we feel more alive. And active addiction does that for us. It can provide the drama of hiding, sneaking, isolating, and being bad around our substance of choice. It also numbs us to the search for meaning. We don't usually find addiction meaningful, but being numbed out helps us not care that we can't find the meaningful in life.

When we give up active addiction and move into recovery, we are faced again with the meaning conversation. How can we as individuals who are highly sensitive to meaning—and to satisfaction—find meaning in our lives without drama and anesthetic? Entering into this inquiry and resolving it for ourselves, perhaps over and over, is a central key to long-term abstinence, to being happy and free.

107
CREATING A DEEPLY SATISFYING LIFE SUPPORTS RECOVERY

If we're going to succeed in recovery, we have to create something new for ourselves. As we've seen, we need a life that is less stressful so that we aren't overeating to get relief from the stress. We may also need a life that is less lonely, that we need to find our soothing through deeper connection with friends or family. We may need a life with less restlessness and boredom, a life that we find more meaningful and more satisfying so that we aren't using food as our primary source of entertainment and pleasure.

All of these things have been true for me. I changed careers, opting for one where the stress of interpersonal politics was greatly reduced. Now I work for myself and deal directly with my clients. No more of what I call "third-party conversations," where someone comes into your office and wants to badmouth a boss or coworker.

Then I began to seek activities that were truly satisfying for me. These have turned out to be painting and writing. These engage my brain and heart in very meaningful ways. I always also have new things to learn and skills to acquire in these activities. Most importantly, I find great joy in the making.

Through those creative activities, I began to meet people who were of like mind and spirit. Our conversations got deeper, more interesting. We worked at solving problems together, at supporting each other. I came out of isolation and began to be more vulnerable with some of these friends, soothing that need for connection that I kept trying to find through food.

These changes have helped me build a sustainable and satisfying life between meals. Without them, my recovery from addiction would be, I believe, less stable, less real to me.

108
MORE ABOUT MEANING AND SATISFACTION IN RECOVERY

Creating a meaningful life with satisfying activities can help alleviate some of the boredom, the restlessness, the discontent we feel. When I spend an hour in the morning painting or writing, my whole day goes better. I've had a deeply meaningful experience that satisfied me and if the rest of my day isn't so meaningful or satisfying, I'm okay with that. I can handle a tedious paid project in the afternoon or irritating traffic or a sense of being at loose ends late in the day. I can think back to that meaningful experience and know that I can have another one tomorrow or right now if I want it.

Spending time with my two closest friends is also a part of that *meaning and satisfaction plan* for me. When I've had time with one or both, when we've had deep laughter, deep conversation, deep mutual caring, that carries me on into my week as well.

Learning something new is another meaningful experience for me. I like taking a class from time to time on something that interests me. Being in nature is also a wonderful antidote to much of what ails me.

Service to others is deeply meaningful for many of us, whether it's watching out for an elderly neighbor, participating in 12-Step meetings, or volunteering in the community. Teaching can be a good source of meaning and satisfaction. We have a strong need to help and share, and satisfying that need can get out us of our heads and more into our hearts.

In these activities, I'm looking to be fully engaged in what I'm doing. My brain is a helpful organ but when it's at loose ends, I'm more likely to act out in unhealthy ways, especially with food. When I find those things that deeply engage me, I hang on to them for I know they're a critical piece of my recovery.

Finding which experiences are most meaningful for you may take some effort. There's no one size fits all. For me, one path is painting and writing. They weren't obvious to me when I stepped into recovery. In fact, my artistic inclinations as a child (all children have them) had been squashed by teachers who told me I had no talent. So I had long given up on myself as a creative. But once I discovered these activities through classes with encouraging teachers, I began to write and paint regularly. I discovered that when I do them regularly, usually several times a week, I'm more content over all. When I'm content, demon food isn't a temptation.

109
WHY THE MEANINGFUL IS SO IMPORTANT TO MY RECOVERY

The more immersed I became in seeking the meaningful through creativity, the more I came to realize that one of my life purposes is encouraging anyone and everyone to express themselves creatively. Not just through art forms, though they're terrific fun for some of us, but through whatever interests you: cooking, gardening, volunteer work, problem-solving. We need these things to satisfy those deep longings for connection, both emotional and spiritual, with ourselves and with others.

And here's the connection for me to sugar and food addiction recovery. When I'm doing things that are satisfying and meaningful (painting, writing a book, talking with a close friend, teaching or attending a workshop on something of interest to me), when my mind/body/spirit is engaged fully in what I'm doing, food is the last thing on my mind. For example, I'll often take tea to my studio but I never touch it. I never even think about it because I'm so caught up in what I am doing. Even more important, I'm happy and satisfied with what I am doing.

Identifying and practicing meaningful activities, whatever they might be for us, are, I believe, an important support and antidote for compulsive overeating. It isn't a simple one-for-one trade-off. One of eating's big seductions is that with food, we can satisfy ourselves so quickly and easily, and choosing to practice a meaningful activity takes time. It can require other people, another location, setting things up. So it isn't a way to ride out a craving. But offering ourselves frequent experiences of the meaningful soothes something deep within us and is so worth doing.

It is also possible to arrange brief meaningful experiences. I can't stop in the middle of a work project to go to the studio, but I can keep a small drawing project set up in the living room, where I can go for 5-10 minutes. It isn't as delicious as two hours in the studio, but it will serve me better than a trip to the refrigerator.

110
SOME OF WHAT WORKS FOR ME

Here are some big and little meaningful experiences that I can arrange for myself:
- Read a novel that sucks me in and makes time disappear.
- Get on the porch swing and pet Mr. Sam, my swing-loving cat.
- Play a favorite song on my iPod and really listen (or sing along).
- Call a friend and listen to what's up for them.
- Write a card of appreciation to someone I know.
- Go to my studio and paint.
- Go for a stroll around the neighborhood with my smart phone and take pictures.
- Work on a collage.
- Look at pictures of art.
- Write in my journal.
- Spend 10 minutes reading on a favorite website or blog post.
- Draw something.
- Be of service: let someone into traffic, make eye contact with a homeless person, go to a 12-Step meeting and really listen.
- Do volunteer work that satisfies my need to make a meaningful contribution.
- Do paid work that satisfies my need to make a meaningful contribution.

111
PLANNING FOR THE MEANINGFUL

A while back, I found this quote: "You put the things you really want to do in your calendar." And that gave me pause. In my calendar, I was listing dates with my gym buddy, medical and dental appointments, meetings with clients, and work project deadlines. If I had tickets to an event, I listed those too and dates with friends—all well and good.

But I wasn't putting into my calendar writing time and studio time, reflection time, reading time, resting time even though, in many ways, those are far more important to me than the things I had been entering into the calendar. I was still just fitting them in around the edges of my life. But if I'm taking my recovery seriously, if it's my #1 priority, then allotting time for meaningful experiences is crucial.

In her book *Slow Time*, Waverly Fitzgerald makes a nice distinction between *minutes* and *moments*. Minutes are measures of time going by, a convenient commodity for talking about time. But moments are something else entirely. They are experiences, events, feelings, connections. Magic moments. Taking a moment together. A moment of silence. A shared moment. They are a point in time. Sometimes they are a ritual. Sometimes they are a surprise.

When I'm in hurry-up mode, like I was yesterday, I am living in the minutes, panicking about the racing time and a deadline. I'm not available to the moments; I'm not present to them. And that's the shift I'm now making. To be living in the moment, not in the minutes. This is what paying attention is all about.

So each day now, I look ahead to the meaningful moments that I can arrange. Is it a phone call or email to someone I love? Is it additional quiet time in the morning before I start my day? Is it an hour in the studio after work? It's up to me to make sure that those moments of satisfaction are coming just as steadily as my three meals.

112
SOME OF HOW I KEEP THE MEANINGFUL FRONT AND CENTER IN MY RECOVERY

- I play with paints and pencils several times a week. The more I do that, the happier I am.
- I write in my journal every day. I record my thoughts and feelings, my successes and struggles.
- I connect with my best friend nearly every day by email. We see each other at least once a week.
- I meditate every morning for 15 minutes right after I get up (and feed my cats).
- I walk most days and go to the gym a minimum of three days a week for cardio and weight lifting.
- I pay careful attention to my stress levels, taking note of whom and what stresses me. I make adjustments as needed.
- I pay careful attention to my tendency to isolate. Since I work at home and live alone, I make sure I have dates and appointments in my calendar at least 3 to 4 times a week.
- I keep soothing activities readily available at home: an art project in progress, my coloring book and pencils out and ready, a jigsaw puzzle or a deck of cards.
- I listen to more music.
- In the warmer weather, I spend time out on my terrace (it sits near the branches of an ancient cherry tree) writing or reading or practicing petitation (petting meditation).
- I do everything with plenty of time. Being late or in a hurry is a huge stressor for me.
- I put meaningful and satisfying activities into each day.

CANDY GIRL

FOOD FOR THOUGHT

106 What do you currently find meaningful in your life? Where might you find or create more meaning?

107 What is currently satisfying in your life? What might add more satisfaction?

108 Where do you feel satisfaction in your body?

109 What kind of meaningful experiences have you had where you forgot about food?

110 How do you register "meaningful" when you experience it?

111 How can you use your calendar to support your recovery?

112 What would be on *your* meaningful activities list?

TOOLS FOR CHANGE

Using your list from #112, begin exploring meaningful activities that can engage your heart and mind and shift your attention from food.

WE COMMIT TO CHANGING OUR RELATIONSHIP WITH FOOD

It's very humbling to feel how much I want to just EAT sometimes, how much food is—and unconscious overeating—is a set of behaviors I have ingrained in me that can still seem so desirable and I can so easily forget the real consequences. Like having a drunken boyfriend I've kicked out of the house, whom I still compulsively think about and I want to call him and meet up again. Maybe it will be different. Maybe I didn't give him a fair shake last time. Maybe just one more time? Maybe this time it will be different...

—Lilian Gael, long-time veteran of the overeating wars

113
WE CAN TAKE CHARGE OF OUR FOOD

It may seem funny to start off this section talking about who's in charge of your food. "I am!" we would all say. But deep in our hearts, we know that we have all given away our power over what we eat. I'm not talking about when we were very small and our caregivers fed us. I'm talking about that family picnic where you didn't want to insult Aunt Fran by not eating her fried chicken. Or that time you didn't want to hurt Grandma's feelings and so you had three pieces of her German chocolate cake on your birthday and then took home the rest and ate it before bedtime. I'm talking about the party you went to given by your husband's boss where you needed to eat lots of everything so your husband would look like a better candidate for promotion.

But if we are going to be successful in food recovery, we have to take back our power and be in charge of our food. Every meal, every bite. We have to find ways to say, "Grandma, you know how I love your cake but I have some health issues and I can't eat cake right now. How about if I bring strawberries and pineapple?" Or "Honey, I'm not going to eat at your boss's party. I'm going to have dinner before I go."

When we're in charge, we ask for what we need in restaurants. We check the menu online, we call ahead and ask about alternate ways of preparing things or what healthier option might be available than what's on the menu. We go someplace else if the chef can't accommodate us.

When we're in charge, we take our lunch to a gathering if it's easier than explaining to the hostess. It's our health that's at stake here: our physical health, yes, but also our mental and emotional health. That's what recovery focuses on: our mental and emotional freedom from the chains of addiction.

When we're in charge, we may choose to eat before we go to a dinner or party. My Bright Line Eating program suggests that we focus on the people at the party, not the food, and that we get to know at least three or four new folks and stay away from the food table. If we've already had our meal, then we won't eat anything, and it's perfectly okay not to eat anything at a function. It may feel odd but it's not. It's a healthy choice we can make. Our well-being depends on it.

When we're in charge, we negotiate with our family or roommate about what foods are kept in the house and where. We don't force our routine on anyone else but we ask for help in keeping ourselves safe from relapse.

114
WE CAN EAT WELL EVEN WITH MINIMAL COOKING

I'm not much of a cook (I think of myself more as a food fixer), but that doesn't stop me from eating three great meals a day. I've learned to fix foods ahead and purchase some prepared foods from the deli at the organic store I shop in, and I am always ready to eat in about 10 minutes. I cook one day a week, usually the afternoon of the day that I shop.

First, I make a big pan of roasted or baked vegetables. Washing and chopping and seasoning them takes 15 minutes; they're in the oven for another 45-60 minutes. In the same prep session, I load up my slow cooker with veggies and canned organic beans and seasonings and organic boxed broth and set it cooking. In hot weather, I put the slow cooker out on the terrace. I wash any veggies for salad and store them in the fridge. I keep meat on hand in the freezer (I tend to buy fish fresh), cheese and yogurt in the fridge, nuts and beans in the pantry—protein options

While I don't plan all my meals for a week or even for the next few days, I do shop with meals in mind. Instead of just buying what looks good or what sounds good, I'm thinking 3 servings of protein a day (4 oz each), 20 oz of veggies a day, 12 oz of fruit a day.

You may be someone who enjoys cooking, someone who would rather cook veggies every night before the meal or put together a freshly chopped salad. If so, that's great. I do that sometimes but mostly when it's meal time, I just want to eat.

115
A WORD ABOUT BLTS

On my food program, no snacks means no BLTs: bites, tastes, or licks. We eat three meals but we don't put food into our mouths between meals. This may seem harsh but it's important. Many of us food addicts consume a lot of calories through BLTs. Equally important is the fact that indulging in BLTs keeps us interacting with food at non-meal times, a luxury we can't afford.

Some cooks find this difficult as they want to taste-test their foods. Does it need more salt or spice? But my food program calls for pretty simple foods as it's easier that way to keep track of what and how much we're eating if there's not a lot of sauce. I've learned to make soup with herbs and spices that aren't finicky like garlic or basil or cumin, where the exact quantity isn't all that important. And I can always add salt and pepper at the table.

No BLTs also applies to not eating from other people's plates. "Want a bite?" or "You should taste this." While I'm not concerned about the few calories I might consume in that bite, I am committed to being conscious and deliberate about my food. When I sat down to the meal, a bite from your plate wasn't in my plan. So I just say no thanks.

116
WE CAN MAKE SURE WE HAVE DELICIOUS FOOD

As you're seeing, recovery from food addiction means changing our relationship with food. For many of us, food has been the most reliable form of satisfaction, soothing, and relaxation. We now have to find that elsewhere in our lives, so food must have a simpler role in our lives: the fuel for the life between meals. But that doesn't mean we can't enjoy it. We are wired to like to eat, to savor the tastes of foods, to like sweet and salty and sour and bitter. Food should give us pleasure, just not all the pleasure we ever get. We need to enjoy every meal or we may well go back to eating the old way.

Some food addicts in recovery are frightened of food. They find it safest and simplest to eat the same things at each meal each day. My mother was like that. She ate oatmeal with a banana for breakfast, cottage cheese with fruit or tomato at lunch, fish and a big salad for dinner day after day. And then she would get tired of that and she would start eating anything and everything again.

I don't want that. I want three delicious meals a day. I want ripe mango and strawberries and a good plain yogurt and roasted sweet potatoes and scrambled eggs for my breakfasts. I want a great salad with fresh veggies and romaine or butter lettuce with nuts and chicken and a juicy apple for my lunches. I want slices of lean ham and roasted veggies and an excellent cole slaw for my dinner. And I want something else equally good the next day. I don't want to relapse out of boredom, so I keep variety in my meal plans. And as my taste buds have healed from the sugar overload I kept them on for so many years, I find real pleasure in simple, fresh foods.

117
CHANGING MY DEFINITION OF DELICIOUS

When I was active in my addiction, which I call a "food free-for-all," my definition of *delicious* was pretty narrow. I would have said, if asked, that I like most all foods, but the truth is that I only tolerated most healthy foods. What I really wanted were foods that were sweet and fat, like ice cream or pudding with whipped cream, and foods that were salty and fat, like clam dip and potato chips. I liked the way these foods tasted and I loved the way they could make me feel: numb, sleepy, sedated. My anxiety levels would go down and while I wouldn't call it happy, I did feel relaxed when all that sugar and fat hit my system.

In recovery, I have a much broader definition of *delicious*. All fruits and vegetables taste great to me. I enjoy the subtlety of their flavors. I really taste the meat or fish, the spices and herbs. And it's not all in my mind. When we eat a lot of sugar and salt, the taste buds for sour and bitter begin to go dormant. When we stop eating sugar and so much salt and eat a wide variety of flavors, our taste buds perk up and go back to work.

While I don't think I'll ever like hot, spicy food (I'm a heat weenie), I do enjoy much more subtle flavors now that my definition of delicious is flavorful rather than fat and sweet. And I know that enjoying my meals will go a long way to strengthen my recovery.

118
WE CAN MAKE EVERYTHING WE EAT SOMETHING GOOD FOR OUR BODIES

My family has long had a pie tradition. My sister is great at baking them and they've become a kind of standard of excellence as a party food. We used to have dinner and then pie. But because we all wanted to eat more pie, we stopped having pie after the meal and instead had salad, what we called an NTH (nod to health), and then pie. Eventually, we skipped the NTH as well and just ate pie and ice cream for the meal. That was okay for some members of my family who aren't food addicts. It wasn't so great for me because once I get started on sugar and fat, I can't stop. Unlike the others, who would fast the next day or just eat salad for a week after such a spree, I'd be stopping at the store for more sweets on my way home for another food free-for-all. That's what I really wanted.

Now I don't ask myself what sounds good or what I really want when I shop or eat out. Those aren't my criteria anymore. Instead I ask myself two other questions:

- **What is good for my body that I can buy/eat here?**

  I know the general answer in advance. I know I'm looking for lean protein (clean meat that is humanely raised, wild fish, organic beans), a ton of organic veggies, not too much fat, naked organic fruit.

- **What can I safely buy/eat here?**

  Safe means that it won't trigger cravings, the miserable need for more. *Safe* means no sugar or flour and no processed foods where the nutrition has been sacrificed for seductive flavors.

I want everything I eat to be good for me physically, mentally, and emotionally. I used to buy for my mouth. Now I buy for my whole self. My life depends on it.

FOOD FOR THOUGHT

113 What would have to shift for you to be in full charge of your food?

114 How could your shopping or cooking routines better serve your recovery?

115 Are bites, licks, and tastes a habit you will have to break?

116 What kind of meals would you find satisfying in recovery?

117 Can you imagine getting pleasure out of simple foods instead of sweet or salty junk food? What might stand in the way of that?

118 How would grocery shopping change for you if you were buying for the good of your body?

119
WE CAN EAT ONLY FOOD, NOT TREATS

As you may know, for most of human history, sugar was a rare and costly commodity. It was only in the last 75 years that chemistry allowed sugar to be easily refined from sugar beets and sugar cane, and it became plentiful and cheap. And many of us have gotten fat as a result.

Most of my life, I collapsed snack into treat. I deserved treats, I needed treats. But that is another value that has to be discarded if I am to stay in recovery.

Now I don't eat treats. I eat meals and I eat meal food. Vegetables, fruit, meat, fish, eggs, yogurt, cheese, beans. You'll notice that I've categorized fruit as meal food. I eat fruit with my meal when that's on my plan. I don't eat fruit last because I don't eat dessert. I don't eat treats.

It's just easier for me that way.

120
WE CAN LEARN TO CELEBRATE WITHOUT FOOD

Every culture I've ever read about uses offerings of food for hospitality and celebration. It's a safe thing to offer your friends and your enemies. For centuries, sugar and other sweeteners and white flour were incredibly expensive and hard to come by, so it was a great gift to offer cake to a guest. But now, thanks to government subsidies, sugar and flour are among the cheapest things we can buy, and we've taken that honoring, that intention of celebration into every day. Sweets are no longer a treat; they are a staple of our diet.

To be in recovery from sugar addiction, I have had to give up food as celebration. In previous attempts at recovery, I tried to not eat sweets except at birthdays and holidays. But I couldn't make it work. One piece of cake or pie, and I was off again bingeing and stuffing. I just can't do it in moderation. And pretending I could was agonizing.

So I've begun calling on my creativity and the creativity of my friends and family for other celebration ideas. Going bowling instead of having cake. Taking a trip to the museum instead of lunch. Spending time making art instead of gorging ourselves at the latest Portland dessert shop.

This can be a place of a lot push-back, especially from family. Our traditions change slowly. If the tradition was that only the birthday girl got cake and everybody else just watched, I don't think there would be so much resistance. But in our traditions, everybody gets sweets at a celebration, and our decision to stop doing what everybody wants and expects can be hard. But our health and well-being are so worth it.

121
WE CAN FOOD-PROOF OUR HOME

Recovery from sugar and food addiction is a lot simpler if our homes are free of demon foods. If you live alone, this is pretty simple. Depending on how many sugar and flour foods you have stockpiled, you can eat them up and then step into abstinence or give them or throw them away. I did a combination. I ate all the sweets I had before I moved into my food program and I gave away all the rest—the flour, the crackers, the bread crumbs, the cereal, the gourmet honey and jams—to a young couple in my apartment complex.

If you live with others, it may be more difficult, but it's not impossible. You can reorganize your cupboards and pantry so that demon foods are isolated in one cupboard that you just don't open. If you have the luxury of a second refrigerator in the basement or garage, perhaps demon foods can be kept down there.

Alternately, you can lobby for much less junk food coming into your home or making it a policy that family members eat those foods away from home. This helps make snacks and sweets a treat rather than a staple, and that's better for everyone.

You can ask for changes in your work place as well. At a staff meeting, let the others know that you've learned that sugar and flour are poisoning you and you need to stay away from them, that it would help you to have sweets in the break room only on special occasions rather than most days. Most of our peers know that excess sugar is a bad idea and many won't push back. The ones that do may well be addicts like you. If all else fails, stay out of the break room.

Note: It can tempting to try to convert people to your new way of eating. Most people don't want to be converted. If you stick to a goal of asking for support for your own struggle, most people are happy to oblige. Ask for what you need for yourself and then, if possible, let it go at that.

122
EATING AUTOMATICALLY IS NOT EATING UNCONSCIOUSLY

Making my habits with food as automatic as possible has been hugely helpful for me. I have stronger recovery if I don't have to make so many choices when I'm hungry, if I decide on my food the day before, write it down, commit it to another person, and then eat what I said I would.

Making choices about food is another stressor for us food addicts. A research study of college students in New York found that those kids averaged 174 decisions about food every day. Where to eat? What to eat? What to drink? How much? Have another helping? Offer some to someone else? Which candy bar should I get? How many should I get? Do I have room for one more? Their choosing went on and on. That's a lot of choices, a lot of stress.

For those of us who already feel a lot of stress around food (guilt, anger, shame, confusion, self-loathing, to name a few possibilities), all these choices just pile up. Both my program (Bright Line Eating) and the 12-Step food programs suggest making food choosing as automatic as possible. To that end, we do the following:

- Follow a careful food plan like the one in #125.
- Weigh and measure our portions.
- If eating out in a restaurant, check the online menu and decide in advance what's safest for us.
- Write our food plan for the next day in a notebook just for that purpose. Most of us do this right after dinner.
- Tell our food plan to a buddy or Mastermind group (we call this *committing our food*).
- Choose not to snack or eat between meals at all.
- Eat as many simple, whole foods as possible so we don't have to worry about ingredients.

We keep it as simple as we can.

123
THE VALUE OF COMMITTING OUR FOOD

For years I rebelled against keeping track of my food and weighing and measuring what I ate. Where's the fun in that? I thought. Well, I do those things now and my recovery is much stronger because I do. I write down what I plan to eat the next day in my notebook, and I commit it to my buddies via email and they commit their food for the next day to me. I also weigh and measure my food every meal I eat at home.

I was right. It isn't fun. And in the beginning it was a pain. But it's safer for me to do this. It aligns me with my values of paying attention, of taking the best care of myself that I can. Eating whatever I feel like and however much I want isn't good for my body or for my mental and emotional health. Sad but true. Being in integrity with what I say I want—a slim, healthy body to grow old in—that's good for me in all ways.

So every night before I turn off my computer, I check my calendar to see if I'm eating out the next day, I check my fridge to see what's available, and I get out my little notebook and decide what I'm going to have for my three meals the next day. Then I email it to my buddies. My emails usually look something like this:

B: 2 eggs, 4 oz sweet potatoes, 6 oz banana/berries
L: 4 oz chicken, 6 oz green salad and veggies, 1 apple, 0.5 ounce peanut butter
D: 4 oz salmon, 8 oz roasted veggies, 6 oz cole slaw, 1 tablespoon dressing

I've been doing this now for quite a while. It's become automatic. It's the way I do my meals. It now longer seems hard or weird. It's just how I do it. And I'm committed to using any tools that will strengthen my chances for long-term recovery.

CANDY GIRL

FOOD FOR THOUGHT

119 How else besides eating might you give yourself a treat?

120 How could you enroll your family in celebrating without food?

121 What changes to your food environment will you have to make for a successful recovery?

122 How might eating become much simpler for you? How might you reduce the stress of so many choices?

123 What tactics like committing your food have you been resisting? What would it take to give up that resistance?

TOOLS FOR CHANGE

Devote time this week to food-proofing your home.

124
THE RECOVERY PROGRAM I SUBSCRIBE TO

A while back, a friend sent me a link to an online food addiction recovery program called Bright Line Eating (BLE), developed by Susan Peirce Thompson, a recovering drug and food addict who has a PhD in psychology, specifically the psychology of eating. She is an intelligent and articulate advocate for recovery from food addiction because she has a lot of education and because she knows from her own experience how we struggle.

I was reluctant at first to sign up. It was expensive ($1000) and I was mired in cynicism and resignation about all food programs, none of which had really worked for me. But a wise friend encouraged me to give it a try and I'm so glad I did. I took the 8-week boot camp, began using the tools, and got into real recovery from sugar and food addiction for the first time. I was no longer dieting, although I do eat on a weight-loss plan. What's the difference? I will eat on this same plan until I lose all the weight I want; then I'll just eat a little more of all the same things I eat now. I am committed to following the BLE* way.

The BLE food plan is based on the Food Addicts in Recovery Anonymous (FA) food plan, which is available for free at **www.foodaddicts.org**. FA is one of the several 12-Step programs for people with food addictions. Thompson has softened the rather strict FA approach and created a wonderful community of mutual support. It is also a business and she sells various programs to support recovery. I found the boot camp and the accompanying videos and support systems well worth the money. I have not purchased other programs from her. However, I have BLE buddies to whom I commit my food each night via email, I have an ongoing BLE Mastermind group that meets weekly online, and I have ongoing access to all the videos and other materials from the boot camp. Doing all this has saved my life and my sanity.

*You can find out more at **www.brightlineeating.com**.

125
WHAT I EAT

Breakfast: 4 oz protein
4 oz grains (potato, rice) or
1 oz of certain flour-free cereals or oatmeal
6 oz fruit

Lunch: 4 oz protein
6 oz vegetables
6 oz fruit
1 tablespoon fat or ½ oz nuts

Dinner: 4 oz protein
6 oz vegetables
8 oz salad (vegetables)
1 tablespoon fat or ½ oz nuts

This is the BLE weight-loss food plan in general. I use a scale and weigh my food. If I eat out, I use a good guesstimate and eat only one plateful of protein and vegetables. If I eat out at lunch and don't get my fruit, I eat it with dinner. The BLE program spells this out in much more detail but these are the basics.

126
BRIGHT LINES AS A WAY TO IMAGINE OUR COMMITMENT TO RECOVERY

The BLE program talks about four bright lines, lines we don't cross because they are dangerous for our recovery. If we keep these lines sharp and bright, we will be in good shape with food. Here are the BLE bright lines.

1. No sugar of any kind, including artificial sweeteners
2. No flours of any kind, including corn meal; in other words, no pulverized grains
3. Three meals a day and no snacks or bites, licks, or tastes between meals
4. Weighing and measuring our food both for weight loss or weight maintenance and to take the guess work out of eating. If we eat out, we use the one-plate rule, keeping our portions as realistic and safe as possible.

I have found this concept of the bright lines a good one. Of course, we could call them *rules* or *policies* or *structure*. They are all those. But there's a lovely symbolism of the light, of shining the light on what we are doing, of staying out of the darkness of overeating and overwhelm.

FOOD FOR THOUGHT

124 How might a food program like BLE work for you?

125 What resistance comes up for you when you consider following a plan like this? How could you tame that resistance?

126 What bright lines would work well for your food program?

127
FOOD ALLERGIES, HEALTH ISSUES, AND INDIVIDUAL TRIGGERS

Some of us have other issues with foods that we must attend to. Some of us have food allergies: we get hives or dangerously ill when we eat certain foods. Of course, we would not include any of those on our food plan no matter what other people are eating.

Some of us also have health issues that impact food choices. I have thyroid issues and don't eat soy products. Other people have gastrointestinal issues that preclude certain fruits and vegetables. It's always important to attend to these individual differences and to consult with your healthcare provider. However, no nutritionist, physician, naturopath, or acupuncturist is going to discourage you from giving up sugar and flour and other processed foods. Not eating these foods anymore will improve your health and sometimes quite dramatically.

There is a third category of foods that we need to watch for individually. Most of us are triggered by sweet/fat foods and salty/fat foods and we abstain from most, if not all, of those. But you may discover foods that are on your plan that you develop a dangerous relationship with. Maybe you get hooked on the sweetness of roasted beets or canned corn. Maybe you find yourself wanting mango day after day. These are particularly sweet natural foods and you may have to limit them if it begins to be problematic. Each of us has to take care to keep our foods varied and to watch for favorites that might push us back down the slippery slope of addiction.

128
HUNGER AND FOOD-TRIPPING

Hunger is a natural event. It is our body urging us to think about food, to get some and eat some so we can stay alive. But as I've mentioned, many of us food addicts have a skewed relationship with hunger. Some of us find hunger unbearable and want to eat at the first sign. Some of us can ride through it and take great pride in under-eating. I'm someone who has great difficulty distinguishing physical hunger from a plain old desire to eat something that can be provoked by boredom, restlessness, sadness, in fact, any emotion that I don't want to feel. All I know is that I don't like the feeling and I want it to be gone.

Being in recovery means I have to stay with those feelings, and if they become unbearable, find another way to resolve them that doesn't involve food. I also can't afford to food-trip, to spend minutes or hours fantasizing about the next meal, about the next time I can eat. I have to stay in the present and make choices in the present.

Yesterday is a good example. I had lunch with a friend. She's on the same food plan and we had delicious salads and a wonderful conversation. I'd had plenty of food. But about 90 minutes after I got back from lunch, I felt hungry. I knew I wasn't needing food. There were plenty of calories in my system for fuel, so I knew that it wasn't about hunger. It was about wanting to eat. Our conversation had stirred up some thoughts and feelings in me that I was struggling to sort out, so I wanted to eat.

My first step was to acknowledge this. In that moment, I wanted to eat. In that moment, my feelings were stirred up. In that moment, I could choose to eat or not. I chose not to eat. I chose to go outside and sit on my porch swing. Did I sort out the feelings? No, I couldn't. But I could sit outside and just watch the trees and the light. When the desire to eat faded—and I've learned it always does, I went back inside and went back to work.

The desire to eat resurfaced about every 15-20 minutes all afternoon. It was pretty unpleasant. But I knew I was still not needing food, just needing something, that elusive *something*. I took a break from work and vacuumed. I went back to work. Later, I took a break and walked around the block. What I did exactly isn't what's important. It's what I didn't do. I didn't eat. I waited until 6:30, which is my dinnertime. What is important is that I turned my thought from food (food-tripping) to choosing something else to do to get relief. This is recovery in action.

129
ON CHOOSING NOT TO LIVE LIFE WAITING FOR THE NEXT MEAL

When I was active in my food addiction, food was at the center of my attention. I was always waiting for the next opportunity to eat something I craved. I was waiting to be hungry enough to delight in it. I was waiting for room in my digestive system to put something in there. I was only half-attending to anything else in my life.

After about six months of true abstinence and recovery, I began to see that I was still focused on the food. I was focused on the hunger I felt not snacking, the hunger that came a couple of hours before the next meal on my self-chosen plan. There were some very logical reasons for this. For decades, I had done everything I could to avoid any experience of hunger. As I've said, I carried snacks with me at all times. I had cupboards full of treats and choices.

Hunger for me is not a pleasant sensation. It pushes me towards action: eating. But now on my program, I had to choose to experience that three times a day. Waiting an hour or so after getting up before breakfast. Waiting five hours for lunch and five hours for dinner. It was doable but not easy. I grew weary of the physical hunger and weary of the restlessness that accompanied it.

Bright Line Eating's motto is three meals a day with life in-between. I was doing only the three meals but my relationship with the life in-between was not how I wanted it to be. Food was still running the show. Addiction to compulsive eating was still running the show.

So instead of bemoaning the hunger, I turned toward it. I sat with it for a few minutes when I begin to feel it. I acknowledged it, thanked it, and went back to what I was doing. I stopped looking at the clock every five minutes. I stopped pacing and opening the refrigerator door. I got out my list of soothers and began to experiment with what might help. My top three at the moment are coloring, walking, tidying up. I also turned toward making my life between meals more satisfying and meaningful.

130
HANDLING TOUGH FOOD SITUATIONS

It's inevitable that we will run into tough food situations. If this happens early on in our recovery, it can lead us to relapse if we're not careful. That's why many people in early recovery avoid situations that are too stressful. Recovering alcoholics don't go to bars and cocktail parties in their first months or even their first year. They get some solid recovery under their belts first.

Similarly, many food addicts in early recovery don't eat out for the first several months. We eat all our meals at home and pack a lunch for the office. We don't want to watch others eating French fries or pasta or dessert. We may also want to excuse ourselves from cake celebrations in our early weeks. We love that stuff, we want to eat that stuff. Because that love and desire doesn't go away, we keep ourselves out of harm's way if we possibly can.

But eventually we have to go back into the world of sugar and flour and others who eat what we used to. And so we do our best to shield our recovery. If we can, we alert our support circle to the potential for danger. We email them or text them asking for support. We order safe foods and when it comes, we eat with great pleasure, keeping our eyes on our own plates. We refuse offers to taste things, we just eat our food. Other people's food is not our food, as BLE founder Susan Peirce Thompson says. If others order dessert, we pay no attention. I've found that when the dessert comes to the table, that's a great moment to excuse myself, go to the restroom, and text my buddy. When I come back, it's usually all eaten.

Will we be tempted? Sure. As I said, our love and desire for those foods does not go away. But the more time that passes without eating it, the easier it can get to turn away. And when we go to bed without succumbing to temptation, we can be grateful for abstinence and having made our own well-being the priority.

FOOD FOR THOUGHT

127 Have you already identified some healthy foods that trigger your need to binge?

128 What alternative activities could you use instead of food-tripping or eating?

129 How can you move out of a life centered around food to a life centered around living? What might that look like moment to moment?

130 How will you deal with temptations to slip off your food program?

WE COMMIT TO CHANGING OUR RELATIONSHIP WITH OURSELVES

131
ACCEPTING THAT WE HAVE AN ILLNESS

One of the more difficult things for us addicts to admit is that we have reached a point where we are powerless over food, that we have an allergy of the body and an obsession of the mind that is wreaking havoc on our health and our emotional well-being. Addiction is an illness. It is a physical illness and an emotional illness. In a sense, we are crazy. The way we eat and obsess about foods is not normal.

Most of us are born with a genetic predisposition to develop addiction. Often a traumatic event, one we don't always remember, sets us on the path to soothing ourselves with food. When that trauma goes unhealed, we continue down the path using food to medicate ourselves. If we don't gain weight, like I didn't, it can go unnoticed indefinitely. Even when we gain weight, we don't always recognize the problem and neither do those around us. They may notice the weight but they don't see the underlying issues.

It is powerful for me to accept that I have an illness, the illness of addiction. In me, it played out with sugar, then with alcohol, then again with sugar and other foods. I did not choose this in any conscious way. I just did the best I could to take care of myself. And then I was in it, lock, stock, and barrel. Stuck in it. And it is not going away, no matter how much I wish it would or deny that it exists in me. Recovery is the only healthy option for me.

And recovery can't begin until we accept that we are addicts, that we cannot eat like non-addicts. We cannot take it or leave it when it comes to certain foods or, for some of us, all foods. We need a program and a commitment to stick to it so that we can find relief from our addiction.

This step of acceptance is both sad and liberating. However, now that we fully grasp what the problem is—an illness, not a lack of discipline or willpower—we can move into the solution.

132
IT CAN BE HELPFUL TO ADMIT OUR POWERLESSNESS OVER FOOD

I have no trouble admitting I'm powerless over sugar and flour. I have so much evidence of this that any answer other than a resounding YES would be a lie. The box of fruit jellies from Trader Joe's that disappears over the course of an afternoon. The four Milky Way caramel bars that disappear in under 30 minutes. The days, one after the other, when I consumed a half-gallon of ice cream each day, four and five bowls at a time. The one bite I took of hot pancake with butter and syrup just to taste them, and then I ate half the plateful in the next 10 minutes even though it wasn't my breakfast.

I am not powerless over all foods, but those with sugar, fat, refined flours, butterfat—I have no power over these unless I don't like the way they taste. If I really like some food, then I want all I want as long as I want it. I don't want one bite, one piece. I want to be sated with it. Once I get started, I am powerless to stop eating such foods until they run out—even if they make me feel awful.

When I eat a lot of sweets, I don't want healthy meals. I want salty, fat meals like pizza or grilled cheese sandwiches to offset the queasiness of too much sugar. Or I don't want a meal at all. I only look forward to more sugar. But when I don't eat sugar, I look forward to my meals. They taste great.

When I eat a lot of sugar, I stay at my top weight or regain enough to get back there. I'm tall and that helps, but I'm not tall enough to carry an extra 120 pounds. Eating like that made me fat and then it made obese, morbidly obese. I was not diabetic, just not yet. I was not immobile, just not yet. When I don't eat sugar and flour, I can have a right-sized body.

But worst of all, when I eat a lot of sugar, I am back in the obsession and compulsion of food. I am thinking about it most of the time. Not just what's for the next meal, like most people, but do I have enough of all the things I'm craving right now? Do I have the right treats? Do I need to go to the store? When I don't eat sugar, I think about all the rest of my life.

When compulsive eating is running me, I have no power. It's all about the food. So I have to truly accept that I am powerless over it. If I don't, I'll keep doing more *research*, as we call it, trying and failing at eating sugar and flour in moderation.

133
ACCEPTING THAT CHANGE IS HARD

Brené Brown is one of my favorite teachers. Her books, *Daring Greatly* and *Rising Strong*, have had a big influence on my always hesitant ability to deal with my feelings. In a course I took recently with her, she talked about the adage "Act your way into a new way of thinking," saying that this was all well and good but if we don't account for our feelings in trying to change old habits, we won't get very far.

Recently I've been stuck in my food program. I'm not eating sugars or flours or snacks, but I've finding I want more food. The truth is, I get tired of being hungry when I'm under-eating so I can lose weight. I'm not bored with the food or the routines. I'm bored with being hungry. It's a consequence of having so much weight to lose. It's a consequence of my addiction. But boredom is a real trigger for me and in addition to abstaining and weighing and measuring my food (behaviors) and figuring out what is happening (thinking), I have to be with those feelings and respond to them in a way that serves me.

Eating more in response is not my best choice even though it may be the most natural. To be honest, for a few days, that's what I did. At dinner, I ate more veggies and some nuts. As I suspected, I got fuller, which was nice, but I didn't get soothed. The truth is the healthy foods I eat now don't drug me the way sugars and flours do. They just don't. So after confirming that (although of course I already knew it), I've just gone back to my plan, to my weighing and measuring, to being hungry. Sometimes acceptance is our only right choice.

134
PROTECTING OURSELVES EMOTIONALLY

When we are in active food addiction, many of us are using food as a shield. Being numb from compulsive eating helps us not feel disappointment, hurt, resentment, grief, loneliness. Those feelings, of course, don't go away, but they get pushed aside when we're full and numb and sluggish. When we stop eating compulsively, it's not unusual to feel raw and vulnerable since we've given up that shield.

Just as it's important to find ways now to process those feelings, whether they're from past experiences or current events and relationships, it's also important to find a way to protect our tender selves who are venturing out from behind the shield. It's all very well to say that we'll be so much stronger when we come out the other side of the transition, but how do we get through the transition without running right back to food?

First, we don't do the transition alone. We find support in a buddy, a small group of fellow sufferers, in a community like the 12 Steps or Weight Watchers. If need be, we create our own group, our own community by extending an invitation to others who suffer. Compulsive overeaters are usually not too hard to spot. And we can do this with tact and kindness by asking for help. "I'm finding ways to stop eating compulsively. Is this something you'd be interested in exploring with me or supporting me in doing?"

If we have serious emotional issues to work through, we shop around until we find the right counselor or spiritual director. We have a serious conversation with our doctor. If that person doesn't offer much help, we find another. We may also need to shop around for the right 12-Step meeting or the right Weight Watchers group. Not all groups have the same vibe, the same welcoming atmosphere. Our approaches to recovery can be quite varied, so it's important to find others who approach it in a way that works for us.

Piece by piece, we put together the path of our recovery. We begin to address our stressors, our problems bit by bit, one at a time. If we feel overwhelmed, we back off and cut ourselves some slack. At the same time, we stay the course by abstaining, knowing this is what we really want.

FOOD FOR THOUGHT

131 Do you believe your relationship with sugar and food qualifies as an addiction (an illness)? If yes, how does this impact your feelings about yourself? If you don't define it as an illness, how might that impact your recovery?

132 How much more research do you want to do before you admit your powerlessness over food? Is there anything that research can teach you that you don't already know?

133 What looks hard about recovery to you? Can you acknowledge that it is hard and move forward anyway?

134 What emotional issues do you think may surface as you move into recovery?

135
AVOIDING BECOMING TOO TIRED, LONELY, OR ANGRY

One of the best pieces of 12-Step advice for me was the admonition to avoid becoming too angry, lonely, or tired. This isn't some woo-woo adage; it's based in a very practical reality. When we are too tired, lonely, or angry, we make poor decisions. We are not just ordinarily vulnerable. We are especially vulnerable to relapse, to returning to our old way of coping.

One of the biggest challenges in recovery is to discover ways of accepting, holding, and mitigating these big emotions. If we don't, our chances of heading right back into food are enormous.

Two of these are totally up to us: tired and lonely. Angry is, well, another story.

136
DEALING WITH TIRED: RESTING AND PARING BACK ON OUR SCHEDULES

We all know that we need a good amount of sleep to function well and to make good choices. But you may not know that when you are eating less for weight loss, you need even more rest. Your body has to work harder than usual to lose the weight (burn fat, flush the toxins that are in the fat, build muscle) and it's doing so on less fuel (you're eating less). So as you begin to trim down your body, it's also important to trim down your schedule.

Many of us find that when we are altering our food, this is a good time to stop eating out for a while. We want to get used to the kinds of foods and the amounts of food that are good for us, and we want to remove ourselves from tempting demon foods until we build up strength and new habits, so it's just easier to do that at home. Just as important, not eating out also means less coming and going and fewer people to interact with during whatever detox experience we are having. We may want to limit our activities to maintenance for ourselves and our family (shopping, necessary errands) and just rest in-between.

For the first several months, it may be a good idea to go to bed an hour earlier or to take a nap on your days off. Just sitting quietly for a while, with a book or without, can help us restore our energy.

137
IDEAS FOR MORE AND BETTER REST

- If you have a TV in your bedroom, move it to another room. TV right before bed disrupts sound sleep. If you can't move it, put a cloth over it.
- Leave other electronics in another room as well. Studies have shown that having your laptop or smart phone in the room is not good for sleep.
- A dark, cool room is best for sleep. Perhaps it's time for new curtains with a blackout lining. Some people sleep better with a soft sleep mask covering their eyes.
- Use a sound machine for white noise if you live in a loud neighborhood.
- Turn off all screens an hour before bedtime. Screen lights keep your brain on alert. You don't want that when you are trying to rest.
- Have dinner 3-4 hours before bedtime so that your digestive system can also rest.
- Avoid exercising after dinner. Exercise revs most of us up. Instead try a slow stroll through the neighborhood.
- Read something calming and uplifting before sleep. Or write in your journal to empty your head from the day.
- Have the best bed you can. With some of the money I've saved from not eating sweets, I bought some fabulous sheets.

138
ADDRESSING OUR LONELINESS

Many of us have used compulsive eating to deal with our loneliness. For some of us, that comes from too much aloneness. For others of us, we are lonely even when surrounded by friends and family. And anyone of us can experience a more existential loneliness, feeling that no one understands us.

If you're an extroverted addict, you thrive on your time with others. Interacting with others energizes you, makes you feel alive. So you may struggle with a deep sense of emptiness when you are by yourself. While you may be tempted to just never be alone, this may not be the best idea. Learning to be okay with ourselves is one of the challenges of recovery and we can do it in small doses, if need be. Taking a walk by ourselves, not for exercise but for contemplation, is a great way to start. You can build up from 5-10 minutes to 30-45 minutes. You can do this in your neighborhood or drive to a park and walk there. Connecting more deeply with nature in any of its forms can soothe us, often more than we may realize.

If you're an introverted addict, you'll have little trouble with being alone. The problem may be instead that you are alone too much. It will take courage and willingness to pick up the phone and call a friend or your food buddy. We recovering introverts need to put more social time in our calendars. This is where getting to know several other introverts in recovery is helpful. They'll understand your quest for more connection in a far deeper way than an extrovert will.

As an introvert, I find that my need for spiritual connection is also strong. I connect with my Higher Power through reading, through nature, through my pets. This can soothe my loneliness just as well as a talk with a good friend.

139
WHAT ABOUT ANGER?

Prolonged anger and resentment are dangerous for those of us in recovery. These emotions are so uncomfortable, so toxic that most of us addicts will be do anything to get relief, including picking up food again. Our challenge is to experience these feelings and deal with them safely and quickly.

First, as we've already discussed, we can work to eliminate known stressors. We can clean up our finances, our environments, our relationships as best we can. We can address loneliness and fatigue, which can make our tempers shorter. We can create more spaciousness in our schedules so that hurry is not contributing to our irritation.

We can create generosity and tenderness practices. We can listen generously to other people's upset, bringing our whole self to the listening and NOT responding with advice or blaming. "I hear how upset you are. Help me understand how you got to this place." When we're angry, we want to hear something like this from the other person. We can use these words ourselves and ask for these words from our friends and family.

Timeouts aren't just for children. When we're angry, we can put some quiet space between us and the event. We can take a walk, sit quietly in a room by ourselves, cool off before we address the issue. We can teach family members or coworkers to respect this need for space, to use it themselves when they are upset.

If anger is a chronic issue for us, we can seek help from our spiritual director or therapist. We can take classes in nonviolent communication, ways of speaking that calm rather than inflame. Many of us find that when we get off sugar and flour and processed foods, our moods improve and our patience increases. There's scientific evidence that the inflammation from sugar consumption wreaks havoc on our nervous system. We can take full advantage of the increased well-being from our new way of eating in managing our emotions.

FOOD FOR THOUGHT

135 How often do you eat when you are tired or lonely or angry? What else might you do instead?

136 What happens to your mood when you are running on empty? How often do you use food or caffeine for a boost?

137 What other rest techniques might be helpful to you?

138 What non-food alternatives can you find to soothe your loneliness?

139 What healthy ways can you use to deal with your anger and upset? How can you let go of food as a solution here?

TOOLS FOR CHANGE

Use the 16 Solutions idea (#163) to create a list of rest practices for yourself. Then pick one and put it into place.

140
DEALING WITH POSITIVE EMOTIONS

For some of us, excess positive emotion can be just as threatening to our recovery as anger and loneliness. Great excitement or great joy can throw us off kilter or be a cause for celebration. If we are still associating such celebrations with food, we can experience a resurgence of cravings for sweets and other treats and party food when we are thrilled about something.

This is why if we're smart, early in our recovery we will use our creativity to begin to discover some satisfying non-food ways to celebrate, a new system of rewards and treats. We go hiking with friends instead of out for ice cream. We get together and play cards rather having cake. We explore something new in our town instead of throwing a party. We make a list of small things we'd like to have (as our budget allows) and when we reach a milestone, we get one of those things. It doesn't have to be a big deal. We still celebrate but in different ways.

Big positive emotions can mess with our heads and bodies in other ways too. A period of happiness can lull us into thinking we're cured. Just about as many people relapse from feeling good as from feeling bad. Especially if we have put some time between us and the last binge, we may be tempted to think that our happiness is a sign of a miracle, that our addiction no longer exists. But it does exist. It's still there. It's not going anywhere except dormant. Dormant means sleeping, not cured.

I'm not suggesting we be suspicious of our happiness. It's important that we enjoy it fully while it's there. But it's also important that we keep in mind that it too will pass. All emotions pass sooner or later. This is life. But if we keep eating sanely, we can have more of it.

141
BEING IN AND RETURNING TO THE MOMENT

This moment, what we call *now*, is all we have. I'm not going to go all philosophical on you here, but it's true. The past may have existed but when it did, it was now. The future may exist and when it comes, it will also be now. Now is when we have choice. Now is when we overeat or abstain. Taking charge of your now, being responsible for your now, is the bedrock of recovery.

Now is when we respond to our circumstances, when we stay on our plan or eat more or something that will trigger us. Now is when we say yes or no to what someone offers us. Now is when we walk away from an argument. Now is when we put on our walking shoes and walk off our boredom or restlessness or when we decide to eat over it. Now is when we ask for help. Not yesterday, not tomorrow, but now.

All religions preach the importance of being in the moment, of constantly returning to this moment, this instant: being awake and alive to what's happening now, to the possibilities now. That's why meditation is such a great tool. Meditation is not about floating off into a blissful state, although that can happen. It's about returning to now. Your mind has drifted off? Come back to now. Be here now. Want to improve any and all of your relationships? Be here now, fully here now, when you listen to someone. Be fully present.

Our relationship with now is one of the most important relationships in our recovery program. Abstinence is all about how we handle now instead of reliving the past or imagining the future.

142
RECOVERY MEANS SHOWING UP FOR LIFE

When we self-medicate with food or other addictive substance or behavior, we don't want to be present to reality, to the now of our lives. That's the whole point of addiction for us. We find our feelings, our circumstances, our lives too hard, perhaps even unbearable, and so we opt for escape. Recovery from addiction is about showing up and being fully present in our lives. As one of my teachers says, "Welcome everything. Push away nothing."

I am really good at showing up for my outer life. I am punctual and dependable. I keep my promises and commitments to clients and friends. I get my work done, am generous with my time and with my listening and counseling if asked. But I am less reliable when it comes to my inner life, to honoring the wounded parts of myself, to being available to listen and hold. Showing up for that too is the recovery challenge.

In fact, showing up for everything is what we must do to stay abstinent. We accept the challenge to accept those things we cannot change and change the things we can, as the Serenity Prayer says. As time goes on in our recovery, this becomes easier.

143
THE VALUE AND DIFFICULTY OF GOALS

Most of us who get into food recovery want to lose weight. The 40% of food addicts who don't have a weight problem don't tend to get into recovery; instead, they stay in denial. Those of us with weight issues have bigger incentives (pun intended). We have health issues, real or looming. We have friends, family, and doctors encouraging us. We have cultural pressures to get thinner. So it's easy to make weight loss the goal. And it's a valuable goal. It's very motivating, it's very measurable, it's very visible. Everyone will notice and congratulate us and encourage us. That helps a lot.

But it can also hinder us. Our bodies will respond in different ways to under-eating. Some of us will lose weight quickly and then plateau out for a good while (that's me). Some will not lose much weight at all for quite a while and then lose steadily. Weight loss as a primary goal can keep us in comparison with others, which is usually not helpful. And weight loss keeps us focused on the food, on what we're eating and what we're not eating. Focusing on food is part of our addiction; shifting the focus from food to life is the goal of recovery.

A better primary goal for most of us is to create success with abstinence and recovery. If we sort out what those mean to us and take steps toward them, almost inevitably healthy weight loss will follow. For me, abstinence is no flour of any kind, no sugars or sweeteners of any kind, and no snacks. For me, abstinence also means limiting how much I eat at my meals. Recovery means not eating over my emotions; it means creating a new groove in my brain where my response to emotional hunger is by doing something other than medicating with food. Substantial weight loss has followed these decisions: I've released 81 pounds and about as many inches so far.

FOOD FOR THOUGHT

140 How might you come into an even-keel relationship with your emotions, both the negative emotions and the positive ones?

141 How might you increase your ability to be present now, always now?

142 Where are you good at showing up for life? Where do you need to show up more?

143 What would have to shift in your thinking for you to put recovery first and weight loss second?

144
THE FREEDOM WE CAN FEEL WHEN WEIGHT LOSS IS A SECONDARY GOAL

One of the places where we can put our imagination is in clarifying our goals. If we've been fat most of our lives, weight loss and getting thin have been priorities for so long that we may not know what to do without them. But if those are our only goals or even our most important goals, it's more likely we will turn a blind eye to the other changes we need to make in order to be successful in recovery.

When I joined Bright Line Eating and heard the tag line of "happy, thin, and free," I resonated most with *free*. Do I want to be thin? Yes, actually, I want to be a lot thinner. I want to be thinner for all kinds of reasons. I want to be thin for my hips and low back, which were more and more painful. I want to be thinner so I can be more flexible: clip my toe nails, put on my socks and shoes with no problems. I want to be thin enough to sit in any seat anywhere with comfort. A big part of me even wants to be thinner for the way I'll look.

But more important to me than thin is the desire to be free of my obsession with food. I know I won't ever be free of thoughts of food or desire for food or cravings. After 26 years without a drink, I still occasionally want one and sometimes, though rarely, I NEED one in that desperate, compulsive way. So I don't expect my relationship with food to lose those experiences entirely. But I have peace around alcohol and I am finding more and more peace around food the longer I stay in recovery.

And the "happy" part? When I am clear about food and free of obsession, I am much happier than when I am mired in bingeing and hoarding and buying and storing and hiding and getting rid of the evidence. That's part of the peace.

145
THE COURAGE TO BE UNCOMFORTABLE

I don't like being hungry and I don't like being uncomfortable. This is pretty normal for a human being. The hunger signal is a survival tool. Our bodies say "Eat!" so that we put in the fuel we need to stay alive. A few people like being hungry; it gives them energy, they say. I don't. I find it a big distraction from whatever I'm trying to do. It makes me uncomfortable.

When I was actively bingeing and snacking, I never got very hungry. As soon as I had room in my stomach for food, I ate something. Sometimes I overate and was physically uncomfortable, but that seemed easier than the emotional discomfort that I seemed to feel all the time: anxiety, restlessness, boredom.

Our emotions manifest in the body; they show up as tightness, as nausea, as feeling gripped in the throat or chest. For each of us, it can be a bit different. And many of us are body sensitives; we have a heightened sensitivity to changes in our bodies. We register discomfort more acutely than other people.

Like hunger, discomfort is a signal to make a change. But we food addicts have gotten stuck in using one change—and one change only—to alleviate the discomfort: eat something. However, to free ourselves of addiction and to lose weight, if that is a goal, we have to find other ways to respond to discomfort.

We can do two things: find something else to do besides eat: coloring, cleaning, walking around the block, yoga, dancing, singing, calling a friend. *And*—notice I don't say *or*—we can find the courage to ride it out, the courage to be uncomfortable for our greater good. For it will pass. Discomfort will pass. Hunger will pass. We will not starve or go crazy although it might feel like that briefly.

I do both now. Sometimes I sit with the feelings as long as I can, then move. Sometimes I just get moving. But I don't eat. I just don't eat until the next meal time.

146
FINALLY LEARNING TO LOVE OUR BODIES

Most of us come into food recovery with an adversarial relationship with our bodies. Maybe we've been fat all along and our bodies have never looked the way we—and our culture—want them to. Maybe we were skinny for a good while and then got fat so we believe our bodies let us down. We hate the fat, we hate our inability to stop eating, and so we eat more. Overeating is often accompanied by a need to punish ourselves and punish our bodies.

To have successful recovery from food addiction, we have to come into a kinder, gentler, more loving relationship with our bodies. We just have to. We can adopt what the 12 Steps calls *an attitude of gratitude*. We can be grateful for hands and feet that let us do so many amazing things. We can be grateful for our vision, our hearing, and our other senses that make the world come alive for us. This may sound corny, but it's true. If we live from thankfulness for what we have, things change.

If we continue to live from self-loathing, from comparison with the unrealistic bodies of advertising, if we continue to eat over our imperfections, we're pretty much doomed to unhappiness. One of the great paradoxes of recovery is that only when we admit we're licked do we find the courage to get out of where we are and into something new and much better.

147
FORGIVING OURSELVES, LOVING OURSELVES

Without accepting how we are, I'm not sure it's possible to stay in recovery. As long as I don't want to be *how* I am (an addict with a physical and mental illness), I can't love myself back into health and contentment. You'll notice I don't say *who* we are. I don't believe that addiction is who I am or who you are. It's a condition we have. It's a complex condition with mental, emotional, spiritual, and physical components, but it's still a condition, not an innate human characteristic or worse yet a flaw.

But If I don't accept that I have this condition, then I'm overeating by choice, and I have to accept that I am actually choosing the consequences. In addition, by not accepting the fact that the way I overeat is linked to a compulsive mental disorder, I join in the cultural game of seeing overeating as a moral failing, a weakness of character. I don't believe in that game and I don't want to play it.

However, if I can accept the "what is" of my addictive condition as a compulsive overeater, if I can accept the problems that it poses as real, then I have a chance at finding a solution. I can let go of the blame and take on the responsibility of helping myself and getting help from and with others.

Self-forgiveness is not easy for those of us who suffered physical or emotional abandonment as children. In our young minds, it was our fault, not theirs. There was something wrong with us that they didn't love us or didn't have time for us or that we couldn't make them happy, not something in their circumstances. We carry this deep flaw with us everywhere we go, in our relationships with others and of course in relationship with ourselves. These inner children are the parts of us often begging for treats, for soothing, for comfort from the shame and hurt. Coming into a healthier relationship with them through self-forgiveness and better care is important to recovery from addiction.

All this is well and good but how do I *do* it? How do I let go of my anger, my resentments, my self-loathing? I'm not sure. I suspect it is piece by piece, bit by bit, like every other emotional process. What I do know for sure is that the answer does not lie in continuing to eat compulsively. That will only get me what I've already got. And this brings me back to committing to be willing to change.

148
WE CAN LEARN TO TRUST BY TELLING THE TRUTH

Almost everything that doesn't work in my life has to do with trust. I don't trust that I'll have enough money so I work more than I may need to. I don't trust that the next man won't mistreat me so I have little to do with men at all. I don't trust that my friends want to hear from me when I'm down so I don't call them. I don't trust that I can survive the pain and sorrow I feel so I stuff it with food. But if I'm going to stay off sugar and other demon foods, I have to trust. I have to ask for help—and accept it.

So how do I do this? This is another of those ideas that sounds so simple and seems so impossible. Here's what I'm finding works for me. I created a support group and I open up to them regularly, even if it's the same problem over and over. I tell them the truth always. When they accept me and support me, I open up more. I tell more truth. I don't have to trust a lot of people to be safe. But I have to trust a few. I am beginning to figure out who they are by taking baby steps. And others in recovery, others with the same problem and committed to the same solution are a good place to start.

I also speak up for what I need. I say no thanks when I'm offered something I don't eat anymore. If there's pressure to say yes, I tell the truth. *Sugar and flour don't work for me* or *That's not something that I can do at this time.* I accept that it's okay to take care of myself first. The old adage fits in here: People who matter don't mind and people who mind don't matter.

By telling the truth, by saying what is so for me, I put my recovery first. That's the only way it can work. I learn to trust myself to take care of me.

FOOD FOR THOUGHT

144 Do you need to shift your focus from thin to happy and free? What would it take for you to do that?

145 What will it take for you to learn to be okay with discomfort and not turn to food to alleviate it?

146 What old stories will you have to give up in order to love your body? What actions can you take today to be kinder to your body?

147 Is there anything you need to forgive yourself for? How might you do that?

148 Can you trust yourself to take care of you? Can you trust yourself to put your recovery first?

Being conscious means being aware, questioning your choices and your behaviors, not allowing yourself to lapse into the familiar and unworkable simply because it is what you have known.

—Gay Hendricks

149
WE CAN BE WILLING TO STAY CONSCIOUS

Being conscious, being in the moment, paying attention—all these are what recovery from compulsive overeating and addiction to sugar asks of us. It's not just about paying attention to what we eat and how much or even how we're eating (fast or slow, savoring every morsel or gulping it done). Those behavioral techniques have not resolved my addiction. I can eat a half-gallon of caramel swirl ice cream in a hurry or in a slow, savoring mode, but I'm still eating the whole half-gallon in a sitting.

Instead, it's about acknowledging our feelings, our needs, our unhappiness, no matter how deep and no matter how prolonged, and being willing to sit with all of it without leaving. It's about staying with ourselves no matter what, not taking the chocolate or pizza or doughnut exit off the highway to the self. It's about learning that we can do this and survive.

Survive. This is where faith comes in—faith that we will survive. That our grief won't kill us, our anger won't kill us, our anxiety won't kill us. That our cravings will pass if we wait long enough.

In my early attempts to stop eating compulsively, I didn't address these issues. I only addressed what I was eating although that was a step in the right direction. What we eat and how much of it we eat are critical factors in health and weight loss. And they can seriously impact our mood too. But they do not solve the compulsion.

That's because the compulsion cannot be solved by more of the same. And eating as many nuts as I want or a dozen oranges is still compulsive overeating. We have to find other responses within ourselves.

Abstinence is one such response. Just as addictive behaviors are a response to the feelings we don't want, the situations we don't like, the curves life throws at us, so can abstinence be. But abstinence requires the one thing that we dread most: feeling our feelings.

150
WE CAN COME TO GRIPS WITH THE FOUR F'S

We're all familiar with the two F's of animal response: *fight* or *flight*. When we are threatened from outside or inside, we can defend ourselves in some overt way or we can flee, we can find an escape route. For most of my life, sugar and other foods have been my escape route. But there are two other F's that pertain to addiction. I've had a lot of experience with the third of these: *Fuck it!* While I was in treatment, I heard a counselor say that alcoholics can go from zero to fuck it in less than a second. And I think for a lot of us compulsive overeaters, that's true as well. We don't think, we just respond, and in the ways that are familiar. I'm up from my desk, into the kitchen, and standing in front of the open refrigerator before I know it. It's a well-worn pathway.

Now I need to move into the fourth F as my response and make *it* my well-worn pathway. That fourth F, of course, is *feel*. Feel the restlessness, the anxiety, the happiness, the contentment, the fear, the discomfort, the whatever. We need to find the willingness to feel it all.

151
ANALYSIS IS USUALLY OF LITTLE HELP

Understanding the "why" of our addiction is, ultimately, a dead-end in the search for a solution. While the origin of our addiction can be explained, at least partially (genetic predisposition, childhood trauma, an increased sensitivity), our addictive behaviors are not rational. Eating until we are sick, drinking until we black out, gambling until we are bankrupt, none of that is rational. And rational explanations don't help us stop. Knowing the calories and fat grams in a Big Mac isn't going to keep a compulsive overeater from consuming one. Understanding the mechanics of a craving won't keep us from reaching for a drink or a candy bar.

Instead the challenge, as a good friend wrote to me, is to *ride it out*, not *figure it out*. And here we are again at the brain pathways of addiction and the need to establish new habits and new neural pathways. If we don't respond to the old promptings, if we don't go down those well-established roads in our brain, they will atrophy and fall into disuse and the new pathways will take over.

Riding out the urges to eat can be tough, especially at first. Sometimes, those urges are physical hunger. But if I'm honest, most of the time, they're not a need for food and I know it. As they say in OA, no one ever starved to death between meals.

Instead these cravings signal a need for soothing. And because we have so repeatedly used sugar and food to respond to them, our attempts to respond differently are often met with huge resistance of the "Hell, no, you can't make me" kind. The challenge is to become willing to respond by doing nothing, by just riding them out. We sit still or walk around when they come. We turn our attention to them. We observe and we wait. They will pass. Yes, they will. We do not have to eat over them.

152
WE CAN FIND SUPPORT TO DO NOTHING

When we pay attention, we are in the present moment, the only place where we can connect with our higher self, in what I believe is the mystery of infinite potential. But as addicts, we are often leery of the present moment. In fact, we spend a lot of time trying to escape it. For that is where pain lies, that is where we feel fear, anxiety, restlessness, anger, and sadness. We perceive these emotions through our physical bodies and that occurs only in the now. To bring them forward from the past, we have to pass them through our bodies again, another now.

Slowing down, getting quiet, going within are terrifying prospects for we suspect that the mass of unprocessed feelings from childhood, from adolescence, from young adulthood, even from yesterday will rush in and drown us. We don't trust that we can survive them. None of this may be true but we are too afraid to find out.

It seems to me that all this comes down to a choice: live in awareness or don't. Open up to what is happening to us or continue to run away with food or alcohol or drugs or busyness. Be willing to connect to ourselves or perpetuate disconnection. As teacher Deepak Chopra says, "Since the journey of the soul happens only in awareness, if you block out awareness, you impede your progress; if you pay attention, you build up momentum." This surely is the path of real and lasting recovery. So how do we support ourselves in staying aware, in paying attention?

153
WE CAN LIVE FROM CURIOSITY AND DISCOVERY

One of the most intriguing ideas I've heard lately is that of living your life from a commitment to curiosity. Such a stance creates an opening for many possibilities to occur, a chance to shift from *why me?* to *what's next?* and *what can I make of this?*

Shifting into this direction towards curiosity has been characteristic of my experience with Bright Line Eating. Most times when I've started a diet, I've had high hopes and expectations of losing weight—a lot of it and fast. I've been willing to suffer briefly to look thinner. But this time I'm doing it differently, observing instead to see what can happen if I ride out the discomfort. Can I feel better? Absolutely! Can I have more energy? YES! Can I sleep better? Not so far. Can I lose some weight? YES! Can I get off my cholesterol medication? Yes! I didn't have expectations that those things would happen, but I was willing to remain curious.

What can happen if you find that place of ongoing curiosity around your compulsive eating? What if in addition to willingness, you seek curiosity? Most of us don't want to change our addictive behaviors because we are afraid of what will happen to us. What if we are curious instead?

It seems to me that curiosity is a key to getting unstuck. It's also a way to approach meditation. What happens if I meditate every day and am curious about what arises in my knowing of myself and my Self? And it's a way to approach prayer. What happens if I pray every day for willingness to change, for a way to connect with Spirit?

I can take this further. What happens if I don't eat between now and lunch? What happens if I don't eat after dinner? What happens if I close the refrigerator door or the snack drawer before putting my hand in? What happens if I don't turn down the candy aisle?

Of course, to do this, I have to pay attention. And I have to ride out what comes up. But what if this is the answer?

CANDY GIRL

154
DISCIPLINE VS. COMMITMENT AND THE NEED FOR COMMUNITY

The American Puritan legacy has left us with an enviable work ethic (working hard and being productive are helpful values) and an unenviable tendency to see every personal difficulty as a moral failing. As a culture, we have been very slow to see that addiction is an illness; instead, we collectively insist that if people just used their discipline and willpower, they wouldn't be fat or drunk or in debt. We addicts know better. We know that discipline and willpower alone are no match for the habitual compulsions of addiction.

Don't get me wrong. Discipline helps. So does willpower. They help us say no when we're offered a doughnut. They help us choose the right restaurant where demon foods aren't on the menu. They help us put on our sport shoes and get to the gym. But they aren't enough.

Most of us must call on other aspects of our human toolkit to get into recovery from addiction and to stay there. We need commitment, we need desperation, we need patience and perseverance and support and community, all the things we've been talking about here.

Desperation comes first. We get sick and tired of being fat and feeling miserable. Something in us longs for real well-being. And if we can acknowledge that desperation, we have a much better chance of moving into commitment. In my experience, discipline comes from the mind and sometimes from a feeling of shame. *I shouldn't eat this so I won't.* Commitment isn't about not doing something. It's about choosing to do something better. It comes from the heart and soul; it comes from love. *I want to take good care of myself so I'll choose this.*

Commitment works best in community. When we share our commitments, we strengthen them. And we inspire others to do what they truly want to do as well.

FOOD FOR THOUGHT

149 Do you have faith that abstinence can work for you? If not, what stands in the way?

150 How have fight and flight played out in your addiction? What can you now do differently?

151 When you think about sitting with your cravings or your feelings, what comes up for you? Can you think of ways you could make that easier for yourself?

152 How can you support yourself today in staying aware?

153 How could curiosity serve your recovery?

154 What experiences have you had with discipline and commitment in your life? How can you use the knowledge from those experiences to help you in recovery?

TOOLS FOR CHANGE

Find an alternative for not eating when you get uncomfortable (going outside for a few minutes, 10 deep breaths, text a friend) and practice it this week.

WE CAN'T GO IT ALONE

155
CREATING A COMMUNITY OF SUPPORT

Addiction is a terribly lonely place. We feel unique. We believe that no one can understand the depths of our despair, our guilt, our shame, our worries, and our fears. And because shame is at the heart of our using, we can't possibly talk to anyone about this. To do so would only increase the shame and the pain. Addiction thrives on this, on the secrecy, the isolation, the lies, the cover-ups, the pretending. It's a dark, dark place.

We can't be successful in recovery if we stay in that dark place. We have to move out into the light. We have to see ourselves and our problem for what it is, and we have to find others who have that same experience and have gone ahead of us into recovery. We need mentors and coaches; we need buddies and support groups. Our success will be much enhanced and easier if we don't go it alone.

Shared experience is a critical piece of recovery. First, we need to know that we aren't unique. We need to know that others have been down that dark road and come back into the light. It can give us hope. Second, we need to share our recovery experience with others, to support them and be supported by them. There is truly strength in numbers. Some OA meetings end with the saying "We can do together what we cannot do alone."

I have found this to be true. One of the great appeals to me of Bright Line Eating has been the central place that mutual support has in the program: getting a buddy, getting a small group of folks to talk to each week, being on coaching calls. It all helps keep me aligned with what I really want: to be free of addiction.

156
MORE ON CREATING A SUPPORT SYSTEM

Many of us moved into addiction because we could not find a way to create deep and lasting connections with others. For whatever reasons, our families could not provide that for us, and our teachers, our friends, those connections too weren't the right ones or they weren't enough. We turned to food to feel better. Food didn't provide that needed human connection of course; it just made us—it made me—not care so much that I was lonely and unhappy. If I got sated on sugar and flour and fat, then I didn't mind.

But now, to do recovery well, I need others, their experience and their support. Here's what I've built as my support system.

Buddies: I have several food buddies. Two are from my Bright Line program. We commit our food to each other each night. They happen to be friends who were in FA together and they also bring a lot of 12-Step experience and wisdom to our interactions. I commit my food every night to these women via email. They help keep me accountable. I also can call or text them if I get into trouble or just need to talk. My best friend Sue also does her own version of Bright Line and we mutually encourage each other to hang in there.

Support groups: I have two support groups. One is made up of my food-commitment buddies and we meet weekly face to face as we all live here in Portland. The other is a Mastermind group from Bright Line. Mastermind groups are encouraged by the food program, usually a group of four people with similar goals. I wanted to be in a group with older women who had a lot of weight to lose, who were already convinced they were food addicts, and who had some 12-Step experience. That group meets for an hour each week via video chat.

Sponsors, mentors, therapists: For the last eight years, I've worked with a wonderful therapist/spiritual director who grew up in Alateen (her mother was a recovering alcoholic) and who is in food addiction recovery. Her support in my process has been amazing. I also use one of my food buddies as a coach. It's great to be accountable to someone who has my best interests at heart. I'm now coaching other women who are building a life between meals.

My blog: I've been blogging about 10 years (**www.sobertruths.blogspot.com**) and I count my readers as a part of my support community as well.

157
GETTING A GRIP ON THE 50-LB. PHONE

One of the first things the 12-Step programs encourage is to get a phone list of other members and use it. Call your sponsor, call your buddies, call other members even if they are strangers. Get used to picking up the phone when you're doing well and chances are you'll pick up the phone and call for some help when you're not. More than 26 years in AA and I never learned to do this. Indeed, some of us have a joke in the program about our problem with the 50-lb. phone.

I've never liked the phone. It's not a satisfying way for me to communicate. I'm a visual learner and I count on facial expressions and body language more than tone of voice to read cues. I'm also an introvert, as I've said, so email has been a great blessing. I can do business and maintain friendships without having to call people.

But email doesn't convey our emotional difficulties the way a phone call does; email makes it too easy to hide out. So I know that if I'm going to make real changes in the relationship between how I feel and how I eat, I must give up being so convinced that I have to do everything myself (also known as *isolating*) and be more deeply connected to the people I care about. Each week now I make at least two phone calls to friends or food buddies. It's a small step but it's in the right direction.

158
SUPPORT FROM AA, OA, OR OTHER FOOD ISSUE GROUPS

Alcoholics Anonymous (AA) has been an invaluable support for my recovery from alcoholism, and I still attend meetings regularly after all these years. But as I said earlier, I did not find Overeaters Anonymous (OA) helpful. There's a very good reason for that. I wasn't really committed to abstinence. In fact, I was still looking for an easier, softer way. I wanted to lose weight and not have to give up sugar, and I couldn't yet accept that that wasn't ever going to work. I had more anger and grief to process around that, which I did with my therapist.

OA also focuses on overeating, just as the name implies. The compulsion is wider spread than sugar addiction, and in those resistant days of denial, I couldn't identify with the people at OA meetings who described eating two large pizzas or six sandwiches. I wasn't willing to be in their camp. Now I see that addiction with food is addiction with food, regardless of how it manifests, although I do believe that my addiction to sugar is directly linked to my alcoholism (unfermented sugar vs. fermented sugar is still sugar). So now I find OA meetings helpful and a place of good support. I also listen differently at my AA meetings now. When others are talking about their issues with drugs and alcohol, I listen to their words for the wisdom that I can apply to my recovery from sugar and food.

The 12 Steps are a wonderful way of life no matter what brings you to the meetings. The meetings are free. They are also very inclusive. Everyone is welcome who has a desire to stop eating compulsively.

There are other 12-Step food programs that I'm less familiar with and of course there are for-profit groups like Weight Watchers that have a group component. The important thing is to find a group that supports you in staying abstinent, one that you can commit to just like you commit to your food plan. Having people who know our struggles and who share our commitment to health and recovery is crucial for us.

159
ABSTINENCE AND RECOVERY AS SERVICE

As we've discussed, food addiction, like all addictions, is a lonely and isolating way to be. We live in shame, not wanting others to see or know what we're doing. We pretend we aren't doing it. We lug around a ton of extra weight and that increases our shame because our addiction is visible to others no matter how we behave around them. We're despairing because we can't stop and we struggle because we don't really want to stop. We want to continue to eat whatever and whenever but without the consequences.

When we get into recovery and start to get sober around food, it still seems like it's all about us: our struggles with abstinence, our focus on eating right and eating less, our new way of life. But as our minds and bodies clear, we can broaden that focus from just ourselves to being of service to others. We may get a buddy or a mastermind group to support our recovery, but we soon learn that others need us too, that our recovery and abstinence are meaningful for them as well as for us.

And it's not just our support they need but our success. We each need to know that long-term recovery is possible and we only know that if others are also succeeding. While we are not responsible for someone else's recovery, we can take responsibility for our own and share how we do that, knowing it serves as an example for others who are suffering just like we have.

160
HELPING OTHERS CAN HELP US

The 12-Step programs are founded on a tradition of service, the principle that recovery is not possible without the support of others. We need to ask for support, we need to receive support, and we need to give support.

Since community is essential, each of us must figure out how we are going to get that into our lives. If we join a 12-Step group, we are encouraged to get a sponsor, someone who's been around a while and has recovery that we admire. Once we've been around a while, we are encouraged to sponsor others. We volunteer to set up the chairs or wash the cups, put away books or serve as secretary to the meeting.

Even without a 12-Step program, we can help others. We can talk about our struggles and our successes with our friends and coworkers whenever it feels safe to do so. We can look for an online group to post to and support others who are posting. I recently put out a call on my email list and offered my home for a monthly meeting of anyone struggling with sugar addiction. I can offer my experience, strength, and hope to those who are looking for the courage and willingness to get into recovery. And as mentioned earlier, we can develop a relationship with one or two buddies and or create a small group of friends to support us.

I do this both selfishly and unselfishly. I want to be of service and I also know that helping others helps me. Our recovery is strengthened by sharing.

FOOD FOR THOUGHT

155 What kind of support do you think might best serve you?

156 Which of the support ideas in #156 might work well for you? Would you be willing to give all of them a try?

157 If you're reluctant to use the phone the way I am, what steps might you take to change that?

158 Have you previously benefitted from a community of recovering addicts? If not, can you picture how this might be useful?

159 Can you imagine being willing to share your recovery with others who suffer? Can you see how strength in numbers could be useful to you?

160 Have you experienced service or volunteering as way to help others and to help yourself?

TOOLS FOR CHANGE

Find out about OA meetings in your community and go to one. They're free and welcoming. If you're nervous about doing this, find a friend who'll go with you. If you've been to OA before and given up on it, try a new meeting.

If you regularly go to AA or another 12-Step group, start listening to the discussion as pertaining to your addiction to sugar or food.

Find a buddy this week to do addiction recovery work with, no matter what recovery path you choose.

My food addiction is not just about me

A lightning bolt
Of realization
Crept on me one day last week
And I saw the wider impact
Of my current untamed demon
The resources used up
To feed my endless hunger
In a way that will never work
This is my version
Of the cruise ship
The international flight
The gas-guzzling SUV
No different
And I felt something shift in me
A vow, a commitment
To consciousness
In a new way
And I left the ice cream
And the cookies
For another
And came on home

TOOLS WE CAN USE TO SUPPORT OUR RECOVERY

161
CREATING A LIST OF SOOTHERS

To deal with our discomfort without eating, it can be helpful to develop a repertoire of other soothers. While it's okay to include some more complicated ideas, like getting a massage or taking a long, hot bath, most of us used food because it was quick and easy. I could numb my feelings of discomfort in less than five minutes with candy or ice cream or chips, so something that takes advance planning and an appointment or 45 minutes to do isn't going to be helpful when I'm at my work desk or frustrated by traffic and a craving strikes.

Here are some soothers I've found helpful. You can set a timer for any of these. When I do these with close attention, my discomfort lessens and sometimes disappears. I've also found that the more often I use one, the more powerful it becomes because I'm investing it with an association with soothing.

- Do box breathing. Count to 4 as you inhale through your nose. Hold your breath for a count of 4. Exhale through your mouth to the count of 4. Hold for a count of 4. Do 1-3 times. (You can envision this as a box: Inhale across the top, hold down the right, exhale across the bottom, hold up the right.)
- Keep a daily meditation book/reader handy and read one page slowly.
- Email or text a friend and ask how they are and tell them you appreciate them. Don't say anything about yourself.
- Organize something for five minutes (a drawer, a shelf, a file).
- Run cold water on your hands and splash it on your face.
- Carry an object that has some peaceful significance for you: beads, a smooth stone, a small velvet pouch. Handle this object when you are stressed and imagine pouring your stress into it. Breathe deeply as you do this.
- Get outside for five minutes: Walk, stretch, breathe deeply, sing out loud. Remember to set a timer if need be.

- Find a chant you like. I love the work of Deva Premal. Put the chant on your phone. Plug in your headphones and chant along with it, silently if you're with others.
- Play with a sand mobile or kaleidoscope, paying close attention to the changes in it.
- Rock your body in a rocking chair or a porch swing or just sitting on the floor.
- If you have access to pets, do five minutes of petitation. My cats love this.
- Lie down on the floor for five minutes. Being prone helps reboot our brains.
- Find a piece of instrumental music that you enjoy. Create or record a 5-minute version on your phone so that you can listen to it anytime.
- Make a list (crazy, I know, but I find this soothing).

162
MORE THOUGHTS ON SOOTHERS

One of my friends keeps two large glass jars on a table by a window. Next to each jar is a small stack of slips of paper and a pen.

When she's worried about something, she writes it down on a slip of the paper and puts it in the Worry Jar. These are usually things she can't do anything about, like global warming or the health of a friend. She wants to keep track of these things. She sends loving thoughts when she puts them in the jar but she doesn't want them on her mind. She finds this reduces stress for her. Once a month she reads what's in the jar. She wants to see if she can discard any of the worries. Perhaps the issue has been resolved. Or maybe there's now something she can actively do to ameliorate the situation.

The contents of her second jar are Joys and Pleasures that she encounters. On a slip of paper, she'll briefly describe something good that happened to her, from a sunset to a smile from a stranger. Something lovely. Good news. A nice happening. A compliment she receives. Any time she's feeling stressed, she'll read the contents of the jar to remind herself of all the good in the world that happens to her.

I love these ideas.

163
16 SOLUTIONS IS A HELPFUL BRAINSTORMING TOOL

As I said earlier, about 10 years ago, I started up a women's group to help me change my relationship with money. One of the early members was an astrologer whose school of astrology used a tool called 16 Solutions. She taught it to us and I've used it in all aspects of my life ever since. It's particularly helpful when we get stuck on something and our immediate solutions (those we think of instantly, like eating something) aren't going to work.

You can do 16 solutions by yourself or with a group. You pose a question (such as what are some 5-minute soothers I can use when I feel restless instead of eating) and you write out 16 answers. They can be practical or way-out wacky. The wackiness can be helpful because you want to get beyond what you already know and think things you've never thought before. The only caveat is that they must be doable, although not necessarily feasible. For example, I could write *Take all my clothes off and get dressed again.* At my office (I work at home), this would be doable and feasible. At your office with others in neighboring cubicles, this would still be doable—you could take off all your clothes and put them back on—but it wouldn't be feasible. But we put it down anyway because in the 16 solutions, any doable possibility is acceptable.

If you do this in a group of trusted friends, each person gives 16 solutions to your issue. In a group of four, you'd get 64 possibilities. Then you all give solutions to the next person's issue. It's fun, it's creative, and it's so helpful. The soothers in #161 came from doing 16 solutions with friends.

164
DAILY JOURNALING FOR RECOVERY

In the *Tao of Inner Peace*, Diane Dreher talks about the calming influence of a *personal ritual of stability*. She was talking about meditation for the most part, that most people who stick with the practice find it centering, stabilizing, and calming. But she says, the important piece is not meditating but having a personal ritual of stability, one that works for us and that we commit to practicing faithfully.

When I was young, like many of us, I dabbled with keeping a diary and later a journal. But I wrote only when I was in crisis. I had a dozen notebooks with three filled pages and the rest blank. I was continually starting over. I needed an outlet for my angst and writing often provided that, but I didn't yet know about the importance of practicing things, of using tools under all conditions so that they become a habit.

Author Julia Cameron taught me differently. The Artist's Way program recommends writing three pages each day. She calls them *Morning Pages*, and they are a kind of brain dump. Nothing fancy, nothing eloquent, nothing organized. Just writing out what happened the day before: events, activities, feelings, thoughts. And you do it every day. These aren't pages for posterity. They are just for us.

Now journaling is a personal ritual of stability for me. Is the writing genius? Hardly. Is it interesting to read? I don't know. I seldom read any of it again. It's the act that's important to me, the ritual of clearing my mind, of letting go of yesterday, or sorting through problems, of feeling grateful. It stabilizes me, grounds me, calms me to do it. And it's an additional place to communicate and release my feelings and my exploration of my relationship with food.

165
USING MEDITATION TO STRENGTHEN OUR RECOVERY

Most people believe they can't do meditation because they imagine it to be some form of perfect quiet in the mind. They assume they have to have the calm of the Dalai Lama to do it, so they give up without taking advantage of this wonderful tool for healthier living. This reminds me of something my drawing teacher said early on in my first class with him. "Never compare yourself to the greats. They've had decades of practice. Only compare yourself with other beginners. They're your peers." Good advice in all things that we want to learn to do.

I recently came across a wonderful simple definition of meditation: anything that soothes our minds and opens our hearts. I love this.

My goal in meditation is to sit still for 15 minutes every morning. That's it. Sit still. Don't get up and don't fidget if I can. No complicated mantra. No complicated pose. I do sit with my back straight (with cushions) and my feet on the floor. (I couldn't sit cross-legged on the floor if my life depended on it.) And I sit in the same two places each day: in my favorite chair in the living room in cold weather and on my porch swing in warm weather. That helps add to the routine nature of my practice. Routine helps make things automatic.

There are lots of instruction books and apps and DVDs about meditating but they are too complicated for me. I just sit still and watch my thoughts. When I get caught up in a story of the past or future, I just come back to watching. I don't let it get any more complicated than that.

Recently I come across the phrase *purposeful stillness*. This is exactly what I'm committed to. This is a way for me to practice sitting through whatever comes up. That can be an interesting idea, a laundry list of my to-dos for the day, a craving, a sadness, a resentment. I can just sit and watch it.

Some days I practice *petitation* instead. My cats love it when I sit down and sit still. Often one will come to sit on my lap and I spend the time focused on petting. It's wonderful for us both.

166
CENTRAL COLUMN BREATHING

One of my favorite meditations is called *central column breathing*. You can do it for 2 minutes or 5 minutes or 20 minutes. I always feel centered and relaxed after I do it.

Stand or sit with your spine straight and your body balanced. Do not cross your legs if you are sitting in a chair or your ankles if you are sitting on the floor, unless you are in the lotus posture or a cross-legged posture.

Begin by being aware of the rhythm of your breathing and letting it slow down.

Downward sequence: Now draw the breath in as though it comes from just above the crown of your head; draw it down through the center of your body. Change to the out-breath at a point that feels natural for you (this is about the waist for me) and breathe out as though the breath was moving down and through your legs and into the earth. Breathe in this way five times: (five in/out breaths = one sequence).

Upward sequence: Now draw the breath up from the earth, through your feet and legs. Change to the out-breath at a natural point, and exhale up through your upper body and out the crown of your head. Breathe in this way 5 times: (five in/out breaths = one sequence).

Alternate five downward breaths with five upward breaths. Always end on the downward sequence. Repeat the whole sequence more than once if you wish.

167
AVOIDING MINDLESSNESS OR "KEEP COMING BACK"

The 12-Step programs use the phrase "keep coming back" a lot. We say it to newcomers, we say it to those who've shared that their recovery is shaky, we say it to someone who has relapsed and had the courage to come back to the meetings. We always mean it for them and for ourselves. We know that it's important to keep coming back, to be in the fellowship of support, to realign ourselves so that ongoing recovery is possible.

In the light of awareness as a key to recovery from compulsive overeating, this phrase is also crucial. The loss of awareness is inevitable. Our minds drift off into planning and reminiscing. It's what minds do. But if we can keep coming back into awareness, into the present moment, then we have choices.

This is the basis of meditation. We sit, we follow the breath or a mantra, and we keep coming back to the breath or the mantra. It isn't any more complicated than that. Here's where we have to ride out the restlessness, the impulse to do something, to do anything. Like a dog, we have to learn to sit and stay. If we jump up each time the restless impulse occurs, we just reinforce the old restlessness. If we stay, if we keep coming back, we reinforce the new (another new neural pathway).

We can practice the keep-coming-back idea around food too. To have long-term recovery from food addiction, I must increase my consciousness around eating. No more mindless trips to the fridge or the store. No more mindless extra servings. I have to keep coming back to my commitment to recovery, to freedom from addiction, no matter how seductive the food looks or smells. I have to keep coming back to my commitment to maximum health and well-being, which is not the same as the next tasty thing.

FOOD FOR THOUGHT

161 What additional soothers can you think of?

162 Consider using the idea of a Worry Jar and a Joys and Pleasures Jar in your home. Anyone can contribute to either jar. Or you might create a variation with different contents for your jars.

163 Who might be willing to do 16 Solutions with you?

164 How might daily journaling, say for 10 minutes a night, support your recovery?

165 What kind of written tracking might be helpful as you change your relationship with food?

166 How might a purposeful stillness practice support you?

167 What does "keep coming back" mean to you as a tool for your recovery from food addiction?

TOOLS FOR CHANGE

Choose one of the soothers in #161 (or create your own) and try it out every day this week.

Create your version of the jars in #162 and use them for the next month. Write about your experience in your journal.

Commit to 10 minutes of journaling in the evening. Set a timer and just write about your day and your recovery.

Create a purposeful stillness practice and share it with your buddy.

168
EMBRACING THE IMPORTANCE OF EXERCISE

When I read Phyllis Theroux's memoir, *The Journal Keeper*, I was struck by her compassionate discussion of her own lack of exercise. She asks herself, "What if I saw my body as a good friend that depends on me to take care of it?"

Everybody needs exercise, but I would argue that those of us in recovery from sugar and food addiction need it more than anybody. First, if we have any hope of losing weight and keeping it off, we need all the muscle we can build (it burns more calories more quickly and efficiently). Even more importantly, regular exercise helps us feel better. It can calm anxiety, reduce restlessness, alleviate some symptoms of depression, help us sleep better. All of those effects can give us a fighting chance at abstinence and food sobriety.

Because my body is used to regular exercise, I get cranky if more than two days go by without it. I am grateful for that crankiness, that malaise, because it keeps me moving. Why? Because although I am a regular and frequent exerciser, I don't enjoy doing it very much. Even as a kid with a lot of energy, I preferred quiet activities. I was a big reader, I liked card games and board games, I enjoyed writing and drawing. I'd play kick the can and tetherball with other kids but I wasn't really athletic. I did like to run but I didn't want to do sports. They just didn't interest me.

I finally realized that I don't like being sweaty and I don't like being out of breath. Both are physically uncomfortable for me and I hate being uncomfortable. But that's too damn bad and I exercise anyway. I go to the gym with my buddy (who conveniently lives next door) 3-4 times a week, and I use the treadmill and rowing machine and lift weights. I walk a mile or two most other mornings. I see this as another practice of my recovery, another gift to my well-being.

169
FOR SOME OF US, THE FREE RIDE IS OVER

One of the ideas in a book called *Younger Next Year* really caught my attention. The authors noted that up to about age 40, most of us get a free ride where our bodies are concerned. We just don't have to think about them very much. They move freely, they heal quickly. We can eat pretty much whatever we want and not gain too much weight; we can punish them with grueling days at work and bounce back. We can drink and drug and have only fleeting consequences; we can drive all night or fly all night or party all night and still go to work and be effective the next day. Of course, this isn't true for everybody, but it is true for many of us.

However, once we reach middle age, the free ride is over. The body begins to lose its abilities and it starts to require serious maintenance. It needs better fuel, it needs heart-pounding exercise, it needs weight-bearing exercise, it needs stretching and conscious relaxing. But most of us don't move into that maintenance. Instead we keep thinking that the difficulties are temporary, that the free ride will return. But it won't.

The basic premise of *Younger Next Year* is that if we aren't moving, we're slowing down with death at the end of the tunnel. That is, if we stop moving, our bodies slowly close down and move towards hibernation and decay (muscles atrophy, organs don't function well, we don't slough off old cells and cancer can start). This is a very simplistic summary of several long chapters, and of course it's a variation on the age-old idea of *move it or lose it*. Get moving or become infirm.

If you're under 40, you can take advantage of the free ride to become more fit now because it will happen more easily. If 40 is way behind you, as it is for me, you can accept that the free ride is over and make moving (a lot!) an integral part of your recovery program.

170
GIVING UP OUR EXCUSES SO WE CAN LIVE WELL

The longer we wait to attend to our bodies, the harder it becomes to get moving. I realized long ago that inertia has its own momentum. And if we've been inert a long time, that momentum can seem overwhelming. Especially if we're fat. There's more body to move, to walk, to stretch.

But if you don't do the moving, the lifting, the stretching, the using, the consequences of illness and inability can range from miserable to dreadful. My goal for exercise over the last 30+ years has not been superlative fitness but to keep moving so that I can do just that: keep moving under my own steam as long as I'm alive. My gym buddy and I have a motto: "Ambulatory at 80." I'm ready to accept that the free ride was over for me quite some time ago, and I need to make an effort so I can do what I want.

171
IT'S NEVER TOO LATE TO START EXERCISING

You'll have heard this before. It's never too late to start exercising. And it's true. No matter your age or condition, you can build muscle and improve your stamina. My sister Kerry taught for a while at a YMCA here in Portland. Her favorite class was all elderly folks—most in their 80s. The changes in them were remarkable, she said, including moving from lifting 1-pound weights to 5-pound weights with ease in just a few weeks.

If you're ambulatory, you can begin by walking in your neighborhood. Start with short distances and keep increasing. If you're not ambulatory, check out Sit and Be Fit programs. Check to see if your healthcare plan pays for a gym. Find a buddy who will walk or work out with you. Almost all of us can do something to support our bodies and our weight loss and mental and emotional health.

172
HOWEVER, TAKE IT SLOW AND EASY DURING WEIGHT LOSS

I've been in active weight loss mode for 11 months as I write this. That means that I'm eating less than I need to sustain my current weight. This puts a stress on my body and my body meets that stress, that need for fuel, by burning up stored fat, which is a very good thing. However, when I add in exercise, an additional use of my body's energy, I add more stress. I think of this as good stress because I am moving towards greater health, but I am mindful that it is still stress.

Because of this, I take it pretty easy at the gym, and I took it particularly easy the first several months of my food program. I don't go all out in the cardio portion of my workout (treadmill). Instead, I walk at a comfortably brisk pace, adding speed and incline very slowly. I don't push myself on the weight machines either. I go for more repetitions of lower weights. I'm learning kindness and compassion for my body. At the same time, I go to the gym very faithfully. It's an essential part of my recovery, not an add-on.

If you're interested in working with a trainer at your gym, choose carefully. Many trainers are young people who've always been fit. They don't know what it's like to be fat and out of shape. While they may be encouraging, they may want to push you harder than you're ready to go during weight loss. If you can, find an older trainer who's kinder in their approach and who really listens when you say what you want and need. If not, find a good book on fitness for the out-of-shape and follow its instructions (see #173).

173
A HELPFUL BOOK AND A GREAT EXERCISE

Several years ago, I bought a copy of Rochelle Rice's *Real Fitness for Real Women*. Like some of you, I've owned a lot of these books, read some, perused others, and found lots of claims and not much of value. But this book I've hung on to. Here's why. The photos of the exercises feature two fat women who look like me. They're regular women. Nice-looking in t-shirts and leggings. They don't look like models or actresses. They look like the women who work out at my gym. Ordinary and fat. In the Jane Fonda videos I used to work out to, she always had one heavy woman in the back, a kind of token fat person, while the rest of the class were sleek, made up, costumed. In Rice's book, we are the whole class.

This book promises only a little and delivers a great deal. There are no outrageous claims, just kind, gentle advice about how to get moving and feel better. She offers suggestions for taking care of your skin (chaffing) and your feet. She talks about the many reasons that lie behind weight gain. It's a sensible book, a reasonable book, and a really helpful book.

Here's her *Breathing for Me* exercise, which I use both during exercise and at my desk when I'm working.

1. While seated, begin to notice your breath. Keep this simple. Note that as you inhale, your abdominal wall expands, and when you exhale, the abdominal wall falls or softens.
2. Place both hands on your abdomen below your navel. Your fingertips should be pointing toward your pubic bone. Inhale, allowing your abdomen to expand forward into your hands.
3. As you exhale, gently use your hands to pull your abdominal muscles UP and IN, as if you were zipping up a pair of pants.
4. Repeat 4 times, then rest by relaxing the abdominal muscles and maintaining the length of your spine.
5. Begin again, performing the exercise for another set of 4, and rest.
6. Repeat this exercise twice a day at your office desk or any other time or place that is convenient. Repeat at least twice a day.

174
GETTING STARTED ON YOUR OWN EXERCISE PROGRAM

You don't need me to tell you how to get started on an exercise plan. There are a million blogs and books and programs out there. There are classes and gyms and workshops.

Much of the advice is to find something you love doing so that it won't feel like exercise. It will feel like fun. And if you can, go for it. But chances are that if you're not exercising regularly, you don't really enjoy it anymore than I do. But don't let that stop you. If you're serious about food and sugar sobriety, exercise will make a big difference.

Find a gym.

Not all gyms are created equal. Some are welcoming, some are see-and-be-seen places. Most gyms will give you a free visit and tour of their facilities and you can get an idea of what kind of folks work out there and whether you will feel comfortable. Be sure to visit at the time of day you would normally go to the gym. My buddy and I put off joining LA Fitness because we were convinced that it was a spandex-wearing, young professional crowd. And while that's true apparently after work on weekdays, we go at 8:30 in the morning and the other members look just like us.

Get a buddy.

I've exercised regularly for 36 years. It's one of the best things I've done for my health. I've exercised drunk and hungover and I've exercised sober. I've exercised thin and I've exercised fat. I've exercised alone and with a buddy. And having a buddy is so much better. We encourage each other, we complain lovingly and jokingly to each other, and most importantly, we just go with each other.

My buddy lives next door. We've been friends a long time and I went to the gym for years without her. Then she was ready and willing. We go three times a week and are both very careful not to beg off very often. She shows up each morning about 8:15 and we just go. No choice, no decision. We just go. And we are both healthier for it.

175
WEIGHT TRAINING CAN HELP YOU LOOK BETTER NAKED

Some of us may be reluctant to lose weight despite knowing how damaging our obesity is to our health and well-being. Why? Because of the very real possibility of a lot of loose skin on that thinner body. No matter how much we don't like our fat bodies, we think that saggy thin body will be even worse.

None of us can know if that's true until we get there. Like the rest of our bodies, our skin will respond to weight loss in its own individual way. Age will be a factor, of course. As we age, our skin loses some of its elasticity, its ability to bounce back into place. But experience shows that much of it will eventually reabsorb if we are willing to give it time. Slowing the rate of weight loss may also help give the skin a chance to right itself.

In addition, muscle tone is very important. If there's muscle under that skin, it can help hold it up and distribute some of the looseness. So it's an even better idea to make weight lifting, either machines or free weights, resistance training with elastic bands, or both a part of your exercise program in recovery. Again you can start out slow with quite light weights, learn a few simple routines (the Internet has lots of good instructions and videos), and help your skin recover too.

176
WHAT MY ACTIVITY PLAN LOOKS LIKE

- Three days a week at the gym
- Staying a full 60 minutes every time
- Stretching before I get out of bed in the morning or during my early morning routine
- Walking the other days of the week
- Gently increasing the vigor of my cardio workouts
- Setting some specific and measurable goals
- Learning and practicing ways to get more flexible
- Learning and practicing ways to get more agile (improving balance and the ability to recover from a fall or stumble)
- Taking one day off from exercise if I want it although I'm happy to walk most days. It just starts my day off right.

FOOD FOR THOUGHT

168 What is your relationship with exercise?

169 Where are you on the spectrum of body maintenance? Working on it or postponing? What would it take to get moving more?

170 What excuses are keeping you from exercise? What if you accepted that exercise is a key part of your recovery from food addiction?

171-172 What kind of a realistic and moderate exercise plan can you incorporate into your recovery from food addiction?

173 Give the breathing exercise in #173 a try for a few days. Then write about any changes you notice.

175 Have you ever incorporated weights into your exercise program? You might find you love it.

176 How might you incorporate more activity into your life that isn't deliberate exercise (e.g., walking more, parking further away from your destination, walking to the store or dry cleaners)?

TOOLS FOR CHANGE

Find an exercise buddy now: someone to talk with, go to the gym with, lift weights with, take a dance class with. Someone who will help you form the habit of daily exercise. Set up a plan and work out together.

Walk every day for a month (no excuses) and see what happens.

USING CREATIVE SELF-EXPRESSION FOR A STRONGER RECOVERY

177
HOW I FOUND MY CREATIVE SELF

One of the greatest joys of my recovery has been rediscovering my creative self. Unlike Julia Cameron, whom I mentioned earlier, I was not an artist in my addiction. Any artistic inclinations I'd had as a child died early under the criticism of teachers and my own need to compare myself with peers who had big talent. But early in my recovery from alcohol addiction, I found myself with agonizing amounts of time on my hands, time I used to spend passed out on the couch. And I began coloring. Believe it or not, but this simple activity saved my sanity and supported my recovery. The simple pleasure of colored pencils on paper soothed me. I knew nothing of right brain/left brain balance. I just knew I felt better.

Then after I read Cameron's book and did her program, I started taking art classes with a wacky teacher who believes everyone can draw and enjoy art-making. Working with Phil Sylvester at the Drawing Studio in Portland was such a gift to my overly critical self, and I persevered until I could really like what I was making. I did have one talent—an eye for color—and I could develop skills with paint and chalk and paper to create things that please me. More importantly, I found an immensely pleasurable and meaningful way to spend part of my life between meals. And painting is one time for me when I don't think about food at all. It never crosses my mind.

Creativity has been so important to my recovery that I wrote a how-to book about getting started: *Sober Play: Using Creativity for a More Joyful Recovery*. See the resources list for more information.

178
PUTTING OUR NATURAL ABILITIES TO WORK FOR OUR RECOVERY

We addicts are already creative. We have to be to survive. We are actors pretending to be okay, we are storytellers who create amazing excuses for our behaviors, we paint pictures of a reality we don't live in. So creativity is nothing new to us. It's just that in recovery, we need to put that creativity to a different use, no longer hiding our addiction but rather strengthening our abstinence.

Having a regular creative practice strengthens our natural tendencies towards courage, perseverance, and willingness. We need the courage to change if we are going to have long-term recovery. Working with our creativity gives us safe places to take small risks. Should I put a green stripe in this painting? Should I plant yellow tulips or a variety of colors? Which will satisfy me more? These may seem like small decisions, but risking small helps us learn to risk big, to have more courage.

A creative practice also strengthens our perseverance. Nobody is born knowing how to use sculpting tools or throw a pot on a wheel or build a bookcase. We have to learn and practice until we can get good at it. We have to persevere in our abstinence in the same way, saying no to temptation over and over, choosing the right foods and the right quantities over and over.

And we have to be willing to persevere. We have to be willing to start projects and then to complete them. To ask for help if we need it. To find the time and dive deeper into what interests us. We have to be willing to continue to show up for our recovery. Showing up for our creative life can help us do that.

Finding a satisfying form of creative self-expression can go a long way towards doing all this. You may well be one of the millions of people who doesn't identify with their creativity but you can start now. Maybe you love to garden or cook. Maybe you've always wanted to paint or write poetry. Maybe you've just never thought of your knitting or basement woodworking as your art form. It's time to see if these activities, these practices can bring you meaning and satisfaction and support your abstinence.

179
HOW CREATIVE SELF-EXPRESSION CAN SUPPORT OUR RECOVERY

Recovery is a process. So is creative self-expression. To be actively creative, we focus on the doing, not the product. To be actively in recovery, we focus on the process of living in abstinence, not a product like weight loss.

Recovery is a practice. So is creative self-expression. It takes serious practice to get good at whatever art medium we choose, be it painting, cooking, gardening, story-telling, writing. It takes serious practice to keep our recovery strong.

Recovery requires imagination. So does creative self-expression. Without using our imagination, we won't fully enjoy our art-making and find it meaningful. Without using our imagination, we can't see ourselves healthier, thinner, happier. In many ways, I think active addiction's main characteristic is a failure of the imagination. We're stuck in a vicious cycle of using and self-loathing and we can't see our way out. To have a strong recovery, we need all the support for our imagination we can get and having a creative self-expression outlet can help provide that support.

Recovery means making ourselves proud. So does creative self-expression. While it's lovely if people congratulate us on our weight loss or our abstinence, it's ourselves we're doing recovery for. In fact, it only works well if we do it for ourselves, not for others. Creative self-expression has its greatest rewards in how we feel about what we make, not what others think of it. In both instances, what we do really matters.

Recovery requires finding more meaning in life. An art or craft practice is a wonderful place to find it. Making something of beauty moves us toward peace and helps right the balance of violence and destruction in the world.

180
10 WAYS TO GET STARTED AS A CREATIVE

1. Speak of yourself as a creative. When asked what you do, be creative. *I'm a creative gardener. Collage artist. Painter. Chef. Garden designer.* Who cares if it's just your garden? Speak it and it will live.
2. Put together a creativity box: scissors, glue sticks, colored pencils, glitter, feathers, pretty papers, pipe cleaners, photo-rich magazines, marbles, velcro, whatever appeals to you. Use a covered Rubbermaid storage box. Take a trip to Michael's or another craft store, set a $ limit, and be creative in your purchases. Once a week, get the box out and make something totally goofy.
3. Get a stack of 4x6 index cards, colored pencils, and a sharpener. Draw something in your environment (a cup, a key, a book, a window) for 5 minutes every day when you come home from work. You will get better every day. Keep the cards in a file box and look through them from time to time. Or try a free app for your iPad like Paper 53. I love drawing on it when I'm waiting somewhere for an appointment.
4. Get *The Writer's Book of Days* by Judy Reeves and do a 10-minute daily writing practice.
5. Commit to the 12-week program of *The Artist's Way* by Julia Cameron. You can commit to the full program or just to one portion: Artist's Dates, Chapter Activities, Morning Pages. Many *Artist's Way* groups also exist if you want company doing this.
6. Create an altar. Use a small table, a shelf, a shoebox. Use a shawl, a piece of nice fabric, a scarf, a cloth napkin. Add items important to you emotionally, spiritually, creatively. Change it on an important day of the month.
7. Go boldly into your creative life. Commit to the year program of a book like **Art & Soul** (Pam Grout) or the **Creativity Book** (Eric Maisel). It'll change your life in an amazing and positive way.
8. Spend part of a weekend day in creative mode. Decide for a period of time (I recommend 3-4 hours) that everything you do will come out of your sense of creativity. Stack the dishes in the drainer in

an interesting pattern. Wipe the kitchen counter mindfully and artistically. You get the idea.
9. Collect photo-rich magazines for collage work, scissors, and glue sticks. Use the other side of the 4x6 cards in #3 and create small juxtapositions of images and shapes that please you.
10. Gather a small group of others in recovery from food addiction to meet for a couple of hours once a month and do show and tell with creative projects. No judgements, no critiques, just holding a space for each other to risk and share your creativity.

FOOD FOR THOUGHT

177 What is your relationship with your creative self?

178 What forms of creative self-expression might interest you to try?

179 Which of the ideas in #179 resonates most with you? How do you think creative self-expression might enhance your recovery and your life?

TOOLS FOR CHANGE

Choose one of the ideas in #170 and get started. Make notes in your journal of any changes you notice in your mood and your recovery.

Get a catalog for the community college in your area and see if there's a creative class of any kind that interests you: painting, pottery, flower arranging, cooking. Sign up!

OTHER WAYS OF TAKING CARE OF OURSELVES

181
OFFERING UNCONDITIONAL FRIENDLINESS TO OURSELVES

At a retreat I attended a couple of years ago, my friend Molly spoke her intention to offer unconditional friendliness to herself. When I asked her about the phrase, she said it came from Buddhist teacher Pema Chodron.

I've been thinking about that ever since. Having *unconditional love* for myself seems impossible. I'm not even sure what that is as I don't think I have ever experienced it, except perhaps from my pets, who always seem to love me no matter what. Much as people claim to love each other unconditionally, I think as human beings we have expectations. We may love with only a few conditions, but I think we always love with some expectation, if only for basic decency and honesty. If those get violated, we may forgive and love the person again, but I don't think it's unconditional. That's been my own experience anyway, both in giving and in receiving.

But the idea of *unconditional friendliness* is one I can get behind, one I can imagine living into. I know how to be friendly, to be kind, to be generous. I can choose what I eat and don't eat out of that sense of friendliness and caring for myself. I can learn my trigger foods and eliminate them from my plan. I can manage my stresses and stay out of conversations and situations that aggravate them. I can choose self-talk that supports me. I can befriend my body, my mind, and my heart unconditionally.

182
CREATING A CIRCLE OF WELL-BEING

Recently I heard a woman speak about a circle of well-being, all the things she found that worked best for herself. So I spent some time thinking about the things that I would put in my circle. Here they are in no particular order:

- No sugars, no flours, no snacks
- Being in bed by 10 pm and up by 7 am (8-9 hours a night works well for me)
- Going to the gym 3-4 times a week
- Walking on all other days with illness or seriously inclement weather the only excuses
- Writing 2-3 pages in my journal every day
- Playing with color every day
- Working on a writing project most days
- Petitation (petting meditation) every day
- AA once a week or more
- Connecting with my best friend every day even if it's just a quick text
- Turning off all digital screens about an hour before I go to bed
- Taking a creative retreat with friends every season
- Regular sessions with my spiritual director
- Taking only the medications I really need and the supplements I've determined are best for me (fish oil, CoQ10, vitamin D)
- Getting up regularly from the computer during the day to move around and stretch
- Increasing the amount of quiet, do-little, or do-nothing time in each day (purposeful stillness)
- Staying connected with family and friends
- Having new experiences regularly
- Being in wild nature as often as I can

183
CREATING A REST PRACTICE

Being well rested is a crucial part of a healthy life. This generally involves resolving any sleep issues (snoring, sleep apnea, having no electronics in the bedroom), but it also often includes finding more ways to rest. Our culture gives out honor badges for being overly busy and while it may impress others, it doesn't serve us very well.

Overworking has long been an issue for me. I've used being busy not only as a way to get approval from others but, more importantly, as a way to avoid my feelings. That has to change if I'm going to live a conscious life in recovery from food and sugar.

Some time ago, I was doing a values identification exercise with a group. Rather than asking us what value we were living by, the exercise asked us to identify values that we believed in but didn't practice fully enough. Rest came up for me. I had never thought about rest as a value but I realized it was something I really yearn for. So I began inquiring into a rest practice. Here are some things that have worked for me.

- I take a walk, talk with a friend, or read after lunch instead of getting busy immediately again.
- I plan 90 minutes for lunch with a friend or client: plenty of time to get there, be there, and come back.
- When my cats ask for my attention, I stop what I'm doing and give it to them, whole-heartedly.
- I do my best not to multi-task. It's a misnomer anyway. We can only focus on one thing at a time; multi-tasking is continually flipping from one focus to another, giving neither our full attention. Now when I'm on the phone, I turn away from the computer or go into another room, where I can give the caller my attention. I'm starting to look for all kinds of ways in which I can pay fuller attention.
- Stopping in the middle of a work morning to go outside and just be for a few minutes
- Watching less TV and painting or reading more
- Being on my porch swing
- Naps

184
USING OR NOT USING THE SCALE

For years I didn't own a scale. I was just getting fatter and fatter, and I didn't want to know. My clothes were a good enough indicator as I went from XL to 1X to 2X to 3X. When I finally accepted that I was a food addict, I was contemplating 4X for any new clothes.

Part of my recovery from food addiction is knowing the truth, the whole truth, and nothing but the truth about my food and its effects on me. So when I found the Bright Line program, I bought a digital scale and I also had a friend take all my measurements: bust, waist, chest, hips, thighs, neck, wrist, upper arm, calves. I weigh myself once or twice a week and keep track on a free phone app called Just Weight.

Some people don't do well with the scale. They obsess about the numbers. My friend Lily, who's a food addict, does that. She's better off using a particular pair of jeans as her weight indicator. So if you get obsessed by the ups and downs, you might want to use the scale once a month. If you're on a healthy weight-loss plan, you should see lower numbers each month.

BLE originator Susan Peirce Thompson encourages her program participants to focus on the program: no sugars, no flours, no snacks, weighing and eating appropriate amounts of healthy foods. If we focus on the program, we will lose weight, she says. If we focus on losing weight, we will lose the program. I find this good advice.

I have also found it helpful to see the scale as a relative indicator, not an absolute. As long as the trend is generally down, less weight, I'm good. It also helps me to find it humorous. The few times I've tried weighing every day, the vacillations became ludicrous: 221 one day, 225 the next, then 223, then 226, then 220. So I laugh it off, stay sure I'm weighing my food correctly, and have faith.

185
A WORD ABOUT BEING WEIGHED AT THE DOCTOR'S

Recently, I had an appointment to see my doctor because I'd been enjoying the discomfort of plantar fasciitis and I needed to see her before I could get an appointment with my physical therapist. I knew Michelle, the medical assistant, was going to want to weigh me. She always does. This is usually a discouraging experience for me. The doctor's scale is considerably heavier than mine (about 7 pounds) even though mine is new and digital. And I knew that going through the emotional ups and downs of the scale's ups and downs was not going to make me feel better. So I told Michelle that I didn't want to know my weight and she had me get on the digital scale backwards. That worked just fine. She knew and my doctor knew and I didn't. Everyone was happy.

If you don't want to know your weight and prefer to use other indicators of how you're doing, tell your doctor or the medical assistant what you need. You have a right to know or not know.

FOOD FOR THOUGHT

181 What might unconditional friendliness to yourself look like?

182 What would your circle of well-being look like?

183 What resting practices would be good to add to your day?

184 What would be the most useful scale habit you could develop?

185 How might you ask for weight-loss support from your doctor's office?

TOOLS FOR CHANGE

What kind of simple rest practice could you incorporate in your day? Purposeful stillness in the morning for 10 minutes? A leisurely walk after work before dinner? 5 minutes of deep breathing on your lunch hour? Taking a Sabbath day each weekend without appointments or plans? Choose one and give it a try.

On finally owning my body as it is

Trust is stripping down
To underwear
And letting a friend
Record your vital stats
And take pictures
Of you back, front, and side
Never mind that you'll change
Never mind that you'll be
Less and less
In the weeks ahead
It's now that the phone sees
That your friend sees
The solace lying
In her willingness
To strip down too
And let you see what
She's been carrying around

WE COMMIT TO BEING IN RECOVERY FOR THE LONG HAUL

186
ORGANIZING OUR INNER LIVES

We addicts turn outward to fix ourselves. We turn to external things to put inside us—drugs, food, alcohol—or we turn to behaviors that keep us focused outside ourselves—sex, TV, gambling, work. In addition, the more chaotic our inner life is (the more difficult our emotions), the more we try to organize and control it.

Many spiritual paths recommend the reverse. When we fully attend to the inner life, our outer life sorts itself out without much trouble. We know which opportunities to take and which to refuse. Our intuition, our inner guidance is a constant support, and the battle over who's in charge—the higher Self or the cravings—can cease. While abstinence may look like an outward activity as we step away from the refrigerator or walk right on by the ice cream section of the grocery store or say no to that second helping, it's really an inner decision, an inner commitment. That inner work lays down and deepens the new neural pathways that can make food sobriety our norm, rather than the food free-for-all we've lived in for so many years.

187
THE POSSIBILITY OF RELAPSE

The door into addiction is different for each of us. Genetics may lay a groundwork of potential, but millions of people with the genetics for addiction don't drink or drug or overeat. For some reason—personal, cultural, perhaps physical or emotional—they don't step through that door. For others of us, the door is so wide and spacious that we don't even know we've crossed the threshold. For me, there was no decision about it, just a need to survive.

There were two doors to sugar addiction for me: one marked *Fear* and the other marked *Boredom*. The fear got instilled in me from childhood trauma that went untreated for decades. The boredom came from my desire to find and make life meaningful and not knowing how to do that. In order to prevent relapse, I must now deal with the emotional and spiritual difficulties that arise. I can no longer run away and hide in food or other substances or addictive behaviors. I have to face them, befriend them, maybe even tame them.

In recovery, in all likelihood, you too will have to confront the emotional reasons why you eat compulsively, why taking care of yourself—a very good thing—got skewed into actively harming yourself with food—a not good thing at all. In my experience, if we don't do this inner work, our chances of going back to the old ways are enormous. Sooner or later, we will relapse. Again, the food is only a symptom of something deeply unhappy within us. But if we do this inner work, in whatever form works well for us, we can grow the strength we need to say no to compulsive overeating day after day for the rest of our lives.

188
LIFE WORKS BEST WITH RIGOROUS HONESTY

One of the foundational pieces of the 12-Step programs is the capacity to be honest, based on the belief that if you cannot be honest, you cannot stay sober from whatever you're addicted to. This is important because most of us learned to sneak, hide, steal, and binge, often in secret. We didn't want others to know the shameful truth about us so we became expert liars. Recovery won't work unless we can give up these behaviors.

But rigorous honesty goes further than food. When we tell the truth about what we are doing and how we are feeling, two things happen. We reduce the stress in our lives and we get seen and understood by others, something each of us yearns for whether we know it or not.

My compulsive eating kept me playing small. While I didn't lose clarity with sugar the way I lost it with alcohol, sugar kept me sluggish and unhealthy. It kept me from fully engaging with others. And while it seemed to make me less afraid, it didn't make me happy. And I want to be happy.

Recovery takes action. So does happiness take action, as we align our behaviors with our intentions. AA introduced me to the idea of walking my talk, putting action behind my words, doing what I say I am going to do. Others can count us then, and even more importantly, we can count on ourselves. We can trust ourselves. This is, of course, integrity.

The integrity doesn't lie in the words of the commitment but in the actions that follow. Making sure there's a fresh fruit dessert at a potluck or family gathering. Staying out of ice cream stores, avoiding certain aisles at the grocery store. Keeping my blood sugar levels steady with sufficient healthy food so that my body is working *for* my commitment and not *against* it.

Rigorous honesty, I can see, is not really about anybody else. Nobody really cares if I sneak candy bars in my room at a retreat or rearrange my garbage to hide the wrappers. They might find it weird but they aren't monitoring my behavior. Rigorous honesty is about me with me. Is this what I want to be doing? Is this what I'm committed to? Where sobriety with food is concerned, I have to do more than talk. I have to build some continuity around right actions, and then my life changes.

189
THE SPIRITUAL PART OF THE JOURNEY

In the 12-Step tradition, spiritual practice is an important part of recovery; specific steps advocate prayer and meditation. However, one of the great wisdoms of the 12 Steps is that the definition of spirituality is wide open; it is completely up to each individual to sort out a personal meaning. The 12 Steps is amazingly inclusive: all those who believe in whatever they believe and those who don't believe at all are welcome.

God as you understand it may be a part of the support system you create for your recovery from food addiction. God as I understand it is the Mystery, the Spirit, the Universal Being that created our world. To honor that and to support my recovery, I do meditation every morning, clearing my mind and calming my heart. I start my day with more peace that way. My journal writing each evening has the same purpose: chronicling my day and any celebrations or challenges. I go to bed with more peace.

Being sober from food addiction opens me up to more spiritual experiences. I am more available to give and receive kindness and wisdom from others. I am more receptive to the beauty of the world, be it human, animal, plant, sky, weather. I need strength and hope wherever I can find it, and when I'm in recovery, I find that it's all around me.

190
INCREASING MY CONSCIOUS CONTACT

When I was using food to medicate myself, consciousness was the last thing I wanted. I ate compulsively to get numb, to **not** have my feelings, for they seemed unbearable, whether it was grief or anger, boredom or restlessness. But when we agree to recover, to get sober with food, we agree to give that up and to remain awake.

In the Buddhist tradition, being awake is the whole point, knowing what's going on inside us, knowing what's going on around us, seeing the beauty and the suffering. So in our recovery, we commit to attending to life rather than the next snack or next meal. We commit to increasing our conscious contact with ourselves, with our world, and with Spirit, if we so believe.

We agree to stop running away from ourselves and our lives, to turn and be with them. In meditation and journaling, we sit with ourselves, our actions, our behaviors, our thoughts, our feelings. We explore them to whatever extent we are able. We get curious. We accept that life is only now, not in the past or in the future, that this moment is what we have and can do something with. Instead of waiting for life to go by and the next meal to come, we step into that now and live, as consciously and whole-heartedly as we can.

191
CONSIDER USING PRAYER AND RITUAL

In the spirit of not isolating, of not going it alone, I continue to deepen my emerging understanding of Spirit, of the Mystery as infinite potential, as a space for and a process for uncovering solutions and connections. And, as I've said, I am convinced that being conscious and paying attention is not only the way to access that Mystery. But being conscious and paying attention is a key to recovering from food addiction. Recovery lies in turning towards my cravings, not running away from them; in turning toward my feelings, not trying to numb them.

Somewhere I read that the difference between meditation and prayer is that in meditation you listen and in prayer you talk. To support food sobriety, I want to develop both.

Here are some ideas I have for consciousness, awareness, and connection to the Sacred:
- Do less. Start with 5% less activity each day for a couple of months.
- Hum or chant regularly.
- Write a definition of *deep rest* and post it where I can see it each day.
- Dance to sacred music (try Gabrielle Roth CDs).
- Take a siesta every day in the afternoon.
- Enter my house with a pause, a breath, and a bow.
- Look for the sacred and the symbolic everywhere.
- Make a list of where I feel I belong and where I don't and inquire into the difference.
- Write letters to the Mystery.
- Do a few minutes of reading in spiritual texts each morning while journaling.

192
"THOROUGHLY FOLLOWED OUR PATH"

An often quoted passage from the Big Book of Alcoholics Anonymous starts out this way: "Rarely have we seen a person fail who has thoroughly followed our path." This is true of all forms of recovery. If we thoroughly follow the path of our recovery program, we have an excellent chance at success. People who thoroughly follow any kind of diet program will lose weight and if they continue to follow it thoroughly, they will keep the weight off. But most of us don't do that. Instead we stay on the path as long as it's convenient or exciting or new or easy. Then when the going gets tough, we fall back into our old ways, sometimes quickly, sometimes slowly. If you've experienced yo-yo dieting like I have, you know this only too well.

How do we thoroughly follow the path and stay on it? First, we don't assume that recovery from food addiction is a diet. Diets are time-limited. You eat a certain way until you lose the weight and then you go back to eating whatever you want. If we're smart, we don't buy this. We know that we need to make permanent changes in what and how we eat. We don't buy the quick fix. We know that it will take considerable time not only to lose the weight but to make the life changes that will support ongoing recovery. So we look towards creating a life and a way of eating that is sustainable for the long term.

Second, each of us has to decide what *thoroughly followed the path* means to us. We can find an official food plan. A number of them are good. My main criterion is that the plan include a wide variety of real, whole foods that are good for me: fruits and vegetables at the top of the list, clean meats and fish, beans. I need a wide variety for it to be sustainable for me, for me to be able to thoroughly follow that path. And because I'm addicted to sweets and flours, they can't be on it. Protein bars and shakes don't work for me as the food is too processed and usually contains sweeteners, but each of us must discover our demon foods and avoid them.

CANDY GIRL

Third, our path normally must include reducing our stresses so that we don't need so much soothing. We must also find ways to be happier, more engaged, more joyful and content. For me, that means painting and collage and other creative experiences with color. It means writing stories and poems. It means playing cards and laughing. It means spending time out in nature, even when sitting on my porch swing near my cherry tree or walking in my neighborhood is all my schedule allows. It means talking about my troubles with trusted friends, family, or my spiritual director. It means writing in my journal and learning what is triggering my present need to soothe.

193
MOVING FROM DISCIPLINE TO DEVOTION

I am a person with a strongly developed sense of self-discipline. It began as self-reliance, a trait I learned early. I was smart and observant and I didn't trust that my parents were paying attention. Somebody had to and I decided that somebody needed to be me. I also learned that if I did what I was asked to, the important people in my life would approve of me. So I did my homework, did my chores without asking, kept my room clean. Later, I paid my bills, was on time for appointments, graded all my students' assignments, did my committee assignments. Important people continued to approve of me. They didn't know that I had a secret life where I was totally out of control.

While discipline and will-power helped me have an impressive outer life, they could not keep me sober, no matter how I tried. I know they are not sufficient to keep me from compulsive eating either. Diets are about discipline. Just don't do it. Just say no. Just don't bring it into the house. Just don't go down the candy aisle.

I'm not saying these aren't important things to do. They are. Not responding to our feelings in the old way is essential for getting the old neural pathways to fall into disuse. But they aren't enough, and they will only work alone for so long. What is equally essential is what we do instead, and finding the way to consistently do those new things, to consistently choose the new way of doing and being, is critical.

A few months ago, I came upon a great quote from opera singer Luciano Pavarotti: "People think I'm disciplined. It's not discipline, it's devotion, and there's a great difference." I think this idea can apply to anything that matters to us. It applies to the way I have maintained my sobriety from alcohol: with devotion. I am also devoted to my creative self-expression through writing and painting. I want to be devoted to paying attention and being curious. And most definitely, I want to be devoted to my recovery from sugar and food addiction.

CANDY GIRL

I like the difference in the connotations of devotion. For me, there's something spiritual about it, something loving. That's a big shift from the punishing, militaristic connotations of discipline.

One of my friends pointed out that discipline and disciple have the same root meaning. So I like that idea too. That I could be a disciple, a follower of good health and happiness.

FOOD FOR THOUGHT

186 How might you approach doing the necessary inner work for long-term recovery from food addiction?

187 What might attending to the inner life look like for you?

188 What is your current relationship with rigorous honesty? What do you want that relationship to be?

189 What is your understanding of Spirit or inner support? How might it support your recovery?

190 What would being fully awake in your life mean for your recovery?

191 If you are drawn to prayer and ritual, what might some of your practices look like?

192 How do you feel about thoroughly following the path of recovery? What might you need to make that happen?

193 How does the idea of devotion instead of discipline resonate with you? What are you already devoted to? Can you imagine yourself being devoted to recovery?

TOOLS FOR CHANGE

Pick a ritual in #191 or design one of your own. Practice this ritual daily or weekly for a month and write about any changes you feel as a result.

Most of us spend our time seeking happiness and security without acknowledging the underlying purpose of our search: Each of us is looking for a path back to the present. We are trying to find good enough reasons to be satisfied now. Acknowledging that this is the structure of the game we are playing allows us to play it differently. How we pay attention to the present moment largely determines the character of our experience and, therefore, the quality of our lives.

—Sam Harris, Waking Up

194
EXPANDING OUR REPERTOIRE OF PLEASURES

We food addicts often have a very limited repertoire of pleasures. We probably weren't always this limited. Most children like to do lots of things. But as adult life comes upon us and we accept the responsibilities that go along with it, our list of pleasures gets smaller and smaller until food is often the only reliable thing. Everything else takes too long, requires someone else to do it with, costs too much, is too much trouble. Eating is cheap, quick, and very effective at slowing us down and numbing us out. And as humans we are wired to find pleasure in food. It seems unfair to have to give that up.

As food addicts in recovery, we don't have to give up the pleasure of food although we do have to give up the pleasure of some foods. We have to stay away from our trigger foods, the ones that make us lose control and binge. But as the weeks and months of recovery go on, our taste buds heal and resurface and become very discriminating so that ripe strawberries or a crisp carrot is delicious. Fresh foods well prepared are a great pleasure.

At the same time, we need to move out from food to find other activities that bring us joy, contentment, meaning, and engagement. This can take a while. It's easy to say and not so easy to do. But we can try things out. We can go for a hike with friends. We can go bowling with our family. We can take an art class or a dance class. We can join a group that sings each week or learn an instrument. We can challenge ourselves in new ways. We can do this not out of resignation but out of curiosity.

What might bring us pleasure? What might be fun? And we can be kind and gentle with ourselves and use our talent for perseverance to keep looking. It took me some years into recovery to discover my interest in creativity, but I found it and I'm so glad I did.

195
LIGHTENING UP HOW WE LIVE

Some of us discover that our stuff is a stressor, that we have way too much stuff in addition to way too much of a body. As I said earlier, I got introduced to Marie Kondo's book, *The Life-Changing Magic of Tidying Up*, about a year before I found true food recovery. Once I subscribed to her philosophy of living only with what brings me joy, I really felt my apartment lighten up, and I'm convinced that that helped me fully step into food addiction recovery.

Most of us spend a lot of time dealing with our stuff, mostly just moving it around from place to place. We're constantly picking up after ourselves or our family. What if, instead, you could remove that stressor and get a whole lot of time back for your life? Time that you could spend exploring a repertoire of pleasures? Pleasures you could pay for with the money you stopped spending on stuff that you were moving around all the time?

As always, this is easier to embrace if you live alone or with someone else in recovery. But you can model this behavior in your family and encourage others to join you in freeing up time and money for more fun. And maybe, just maybe, you'll find that this step towards lightening up your environment can help you commit to lightening up your body too.

196
THRIVING OR SURVIVING?

When I was active in my food addiction, I was surviving. I was looking for ways to eat more, be sure I had enough, hiding my eating from others. I was scared and guilty and ashamed. That's bare bones living. When I am solidly in recovery, I am thriving. I am eating well and treating my body with respect. I have time and energy for things that feed my mind and my soul as well. I am open to possibilities, I am open to change.

When I am tempted to go back to the old ways, when the ice cream aisle at the grocery store calls my name and an old memory floods back in of how nice it would feel to be numb to the world again, I'm learning to ask myself this: Do I want to thrive or just survive? The answer isn't always simple. Sometimes surviving seems appealing or like the only option. But it isn't. And in order to choose only bare survival, I'd have to forget all I know about addiction and recovery, and I can't do that. I already know there's a way out. And so, in a sense, my only choice is to stay the course, to stay on the path of recovery and focus on its rewards.

197
STEPPING INTO CHOICE: CREATING OUR LIVES IN EVERY MOMENT

One of the great blessings of recovery is the ability to change. When we are mired in our addictive behaviors, we are stuck in that awful loop of using, withdrawing, suffering, using, withdrawing, suffering, not to mention the scheming and pretending. Our energy and our time are spent supporting the addiction, not living.

In recovery, we are no longer stuck. We have choices as to what we do with our energy and our time, how we act, what we eat. We have the possibility of creating our lives in every moment. Of course, our past choices may still come into play. We may have chosen to have kids, a spouse, a certain job. But we can choose how we handle those things. We can stop, reflect, seek advice, make changes. So much opens up for us in recovery.

This wealth of choices may seem both exciting and frightening at the same time. In some ways, life in active food addiction is simpler. We focus almost solely on our food: on getting enough, having enough. We ignore the rest of life as best we can, living for the times we can be alone with food. This new life in recovery asks a great deal more of us. It asks us to continue to recover and clean up our past and heal, to be responsible for our choices and make new decisions and make changes. This richness of opportunity can be overwhelming.

But we can take it slow. We can eliminate the stressors one at a time, bring in the new ways of being one at a time. We can accept the challenge of change one day at a time, one minute at time, one choice at a time.

198
EASING THE UNCERTAINTY OF LIFE WITH OUR FOOD PLAN

It is a cliché to say that life is uncertain, but it is also a reality. We addicts have a tendency to address the uncertainties of life by numbing out, by pretending we don't care, by dealing with our anxiety in an habitual way rather than by exploring our feelings and handling them in a way that serves us better.

Committing to a reliable, healthy way of eating helps ease some of that uncertainty. We no longer have to have conversations with ourselves about is this healthy? Will it make me fat? Will it give me gas or acid reflux? Will anyone notice how much I'm eating? Will there be enough?

Instead we subscribe to a way of eating that supports our peace of mind. We know the food is healthy. We know we are eating appropriate amounts for weight loss or maintenance. We know how it will affect us. We know no one will judge us for what or how much we eat. We have confidence and clarity around food. There may be many other circumstances of life where we have no control but here we do.

FOOD FOR THOUGHT

194 What other pleasures besides food are already in your repertoire? What might you explore as you expand that repertoire?

195 Is clutter and stuff a stressor in your life? How might decluttering support your recovery from food addiction?

196 How would you feel about life if you were thriving? How would that be different from just surviving? What would a life of thriving look like?

197 How can you adapt the idea of one choice at a time to your life?

198 How could recovery with a healthy, sustainable food plan give you peace of mind?

TOOLS FOR CHANGE

Make a plan for lightening up your office or home environment. Maybe it's 15 minutes a day; maybe it's a weekend with your best friend. How might you associate a lighter, tidier environment with a lighter, happier body?

CREATING THE LIFE BETWEEN MEALS

199
SUGGESTED STEPS FOR ENHANCING SUCCESSFUL RECOVERY FROM FOOD ADDICTION

Here's the truth: Long-term recovery from food addiction is neither simple nor easy. But it is doable and, in fact, it is quite doable. As human beings, we have all the skills we need to do it. Some of those skills may be rusty or weak from lack of use, but we have the capacity nonetheless for commitment, love, devotion, discipline, perseverance, generosity, and kindness. We just need to put them into service for our own well-being.

Here are the steps that can lead us into that freedom from food addiction.
- Clearly understand what we want from recovery from compulsive eating.
- Adopt and maintain a plan of abstinence and healthy eating that is sustainable for life.
- Develop emotional, mental, and physical activity habits that support our health and well-being.
- Create a circle of support that includes others who suffer from this disease.
- Fill our lives between meals with meaningful and satisfying activities that don't involve food.
- Let go of trying to find an easier, softer way.
- Make an unwavering commitment to recovery.

200
CLEARLY UNDERSTANDING WHAT WE WANT FROM RECOVERY

I'm pretty sure that if I don't know what I want recovery to do for me, the seduction of food will remain as strong as ever. So here is what I want recovery to give me.
- I want to have peace of mind around food. I want to eat it, enjoy it, and not obsess about its presence or absence in my life.
- I don't want to worry that what I'm eating is damaging my health. I want it to support my health.
- I want food to have a reasonable place in my life and self-care, not the primary place.
- I want to have a well-practiced plan in place for if and when I slip off the recovery path so that I can get right back on.
- I want to be fit, healthy, and pain-free. More specifically, I want to be able to walk any distance I want and sit in any seat I want. I want to be able to climb several flights of stairs without having to pretend that I'm not out of breath. I want to be free of back and hip pain.
- I want to wear the same size clothes all the time (have one size in my closet) and I want to feel attractive in all my clothes and in my body.
- I want to feel so committed, so devoted to my health and my recovery that what other people eat isn't worth being tempted by.
- I want to free up the time and energy I spend maintaining my food addiction so that other wonderful things can happen in my life.

201
ADOPTING AND MAINTAINING A SUSTAINABLE PLAN OF ABSTINENCE AND HEALTHY EATING

I know that what I want is *food sobriety*. Most of us food addicts who are conscious of our struggle (many are not) talk about *normal eating* or *healthy eating*, But I'm not sure normal eating exists in our culture of overabundance and hyper-palatable foods. I know people who are a normal weight but I've watched them binge and on more than one occasion. I've watched friends eat reasonable quantities at a meal together, but I know they go through a mega-jar of peanut butter or six packages of cookies each week.

I also know that I cannot be a *normal* eater. I cannot eat all foods in moderation. I wish I could. I've tried and tried but I'm an addict. I'm addicted to sugar and flour and how they make me feel. I'm addicted to self-medicating with food. I'm addicted to numbing myself with food. I'm addicted to stuffing myself with food. Only if I go back into denial can I believe that any of this is not true or believe that it is going to change. It is not going to change.

What then? I can be an abstinent, sober eater. I can develop a food plan that includes only real, nutrient-dense, healthful foods. I can abstain from trigger foods and I can use healthy structures to keep myself food sober. Whatever plan I choose must be sustainable for the long term. It has to have foods I enjoy and can easily purchase, fix, and carry with me if needed. It has to have variety and simplicity.

For me, what works is abstaining from sugars and flours, abstaining from snacks, and eating measured portions of proteins, vegetables, fruits, and occasional complex carbohydrates like sweet potatoes. What will work for you may be different but my guess is that it can be equally simple and equally delicious.

202
EMBRACING FOOD SOBRIETY

Being food sober needs to be simple for most of us if we are going to succeed in recovering from sugar and food addiction. Here's what food sobriety looks like for me.

- I eat fresh, unprocessed foods.
- I eat 3 meals a day and no snacks.
- • I schedule those three meals about 5 hours apart given my activities on any particular day.
- I eat the best foods I can afford: organic fruits and vegetables and clean, humanely raised meat and dairy.
- I eat protein, fruit, and complex carbs for breakfast in established amounts
- For weight loss, I follow the plan in #125. For maintenance, I follow the same plan but I eat slightly more.
- I write down my meals after dinner for the next day and share them with my buddies.
- I use a scale to weigh my food whenever possible.
- I use a one-plate rule when I can't weigh my food.
- I keep my environment free of trigger foods.
- I weigh my body on a schedule that keeps me free from obsessing about the number on the scale.
- I am building and maintaining a life between meals that satisfies me so much that my need for self-medicating is dropping away.

203
DEVELOPING HABITS THAT SUPPORT OUR WELL-BEING

This book has many ideas for activities that support our health and well-being and how to incorporate them into your life. I won't repeat them all here but I do want to say a little more about two things.

Open up about what you doing with trusted friends.

When we come clean with our struggles, when we find others who share those struggles, we take a giant leap forward in healing. Talk with those you trust about not only what you have been doing but what you want to do now. Ask for their support.

Commit to riding out the cravings and impulses and turning the light of curiosity on them.

Meditation and prayer are both tools for this important recovery step. Rather than eating or getting busy, when the cravings to eat or the impulse to run away in some fashion come over me, I want to stay and be with them. I know this is at the heart of all of it. I also know that it will help me immensely if I can move out of any internal dialog that says that prayer and meditation are too difficult.

In a recent morning meditation reading, I found this question: *What would your life be like if things were not easy or difficult, if they just were?* And I've been thinking about that. My tendency—and the tendency of most people I know—is to judge everything. And those evaluations color our relationship with that experience and most often not in a good way.

When I talk to people about my food changes, they often want to know if it is difficult. They don't ask if it's easy or satisfying or successful. They ask if it's hard. I wonder if they want it to be difficult so that they don't have to consider changing for themselves. Of course, I' not asking them to change. And I remember from the film *Fat, Sick, and Nearly Dead* that the people Joe Cross interviewed mostly said, "I can't do that. It would be too hard." But starting out believing that sitting with the cravings will be hard isn't helpful to me. It doesn't have to be hard or easy. It can just be.

I will also need to be patient with myself and create flexibility and spaciousness in my schedule. A sense of hurry, a sense of impatience when the cravings come and I'm busy working contributes to the impetus to grab something to eat. Instead, I want to learn to stop and pay attention to myself, to my inner selves, and just be with them in a kind and patient way.

204
CREATING A CIRCLE OF SUPPORT WITH OTHERS WHO SUFFER FROM FOOD ADDICTION

While the decision to eat or not eat and what to eat are always up to me, I cannot do recovery alone. Here is the circle of support I currently have.

I have several buddies, both within Bright Line Eating and without. I commit my food to my BLE buddies. I meet with two local buddies every couple of weeks. My best friend is also doing a version of BLE that works for her and that's a big help. One of my sisters is doing another food plan that she finds sustainable and that's a huge help. I have a Mastermind group of BLE women. We meet weekly on video and share our celebrations, challenges, and commitments. I text or call them in-between if I need them.

I need to check in with someone most days on how I'm doing. I may need to share my food plan for the day or an upcoming challenge (family meal or other eating event). I need someone who will help hold me accountable and remind me of what I want and how best to get there.

While I don't need my buddies to have the same plan or goals that I do, I do need them to be equally committed to and serious about their own plans and goals. I also need a buddy willing and able to connect most days, someone who has time for this. That person must also be a food addict, not just someone who wants to lose weight.

I use my AA meetings as support for my recovery from food addiction as well as my recovery from alcoholism.

While AA meetings focus on alcohol as the addictive substance, nothing prevents me from listening to the ideas and discussions as support for recovery from sugar and food. I might, at some point, consider organizing an AA meeting for those who also suffer from sugar and food addiction. Anyone can organize a new meeting.

I am giving OA another chance.

I have an old, well-entrenched story about OA that doesn't serve me. A friend who recently returned to OA after some years away recommended I seek out literature study meetings rather than general discussion. "You might find what you are looking for there," she said. I think this is a good idea. I could dismantle the chip on my shoulder and start fresh with OA as a possible means of support. A quick search of the Internet shows two meetings at 1 pm during the week, timing that doesn't interfere with my favorite AA meetings, and they are not too far from me. Perhaps my buddy or someone in my support group would also want to go. And there are OA meetings online at all hours.

I am asking all my friends and family to support me in this recovery journey.

There's a lot of shame in relapsing, in saying you're going to do one thing (stay off sugar) and doing another (eating sugar again). And my family has heard this quite a few times from me. But letting that shame keep me from gathering all the support I can is not helpful. I need to keep asking.

I can share my experiences on my blog (www.sobertruths.blogspot.com) and ask my readers for their support.

The more public I am about my recovery journey, the safer I am. Addiction loves secrecy as much as it loves chaos. Keeping my recovery out in the light is critical for me. And I want my abstinence and my struggles to help others.

205
CREATING A MEANINGFUL AND SATISFYING LIFE BETWEEN MEALS

Fortunately for those of us in recovery, the world is full of meaningful and satisfying activities. The only challenge is to find the ones that speak to each of us. For me, that has been creative self-expression through painting and writing. It has included rehoming rescue cats and giving them a good life. It has involved attending 12-Step meetings to get support and give support. It has been working to create the best relationships I can have with my friends and family. It has meant finding work that appeals to me and pays my bills.

It has meant giving up long evenings of TV to do other things. It has meant being physically active every day and paying attention to my food. It has meant reading thoughtful writing and becoming the best citizen I can. It has meant shifting my focus from numbing my feelings to being a source of kindness, generosity, and tenderness for others. It has meant taking risks to change and figure out how to do life without treats and the anesthetic that I wanted food to be for me. It has meant getting to know myself—and others—in a whole new way.

Some of these ideas may speak to you and others may not. Gardening could be your creative outlet or knitting. Volunteering to feed the homeless or read to kids may be the service work that calls to you. Maybe it's a new career or a new spiritual group. We each must find what is meaningful and satisfying to us. I think it's wonderful that so many possibilities are out there for us when we put down the food and get off the couch.

206
LETTING GO OF OUR SEARCH FOR THE EASIER, SOFTER WAY

In 12-Step programs, we talk a lot about our search for the easier, softer way. We don't want to be abstinent. We want to continue to use our drug of choice—be it food, alcohol, sex, gambling, whatever—without the consequences. As I've said, I still want to eat whatever I want whenever I want without gaining weight or damaging my health. I still want to somehow miraculously become a non-addict. And it's okay for me to want that. But neither of those is going to get me what I want to be at peace, free from addiction, and in a right-sized body.

Many of us keep looking though, convinced that if we just find the right diet or the right nutritionist or the right pill or the right exercise plan, we won't have to stop doing what we're doing. We won't have to go through the discomfort of withdrawal and detox. We won't have to be vigilant about what we eat. We won't have to live a life without anesthetic. We keep looking for the easier, softer way.

To get free, we have to stop expecting that such a way exists. It doesn't exist. We have to step into recovery with our whole self, committing to the path we choose and sticking with it. If we veer off, we come back to our path, instead of looking for another path. And in time, recovery will become the easier, softer way.

207
MAKING AN UNWAVERING COMMITMENT TO RECOMMIT TO RECOVERY

In a transformation program that I took last year, one of the teachers commented on commitments (we were being asked to make quite a few) and what happens if we break them. Too often, she said, we invalidate ourselves and our commitment when we lapse (relapse) and we give up. Instead we can have compassion and seek support in getting restored to our commitment. And I saw how commitment and sanity can be the same for me around sugar. How I can have compassion and seek support and be restored to my commitment to sane eating?

First, I need to create and hold to an intention. An intention is not a goal or a task (a doing); it is a way of being. If my intention is to be in solid and long-term recovery from sugar and food addiction, then I will take actions that are consistent with that intention. Indeed, this whole book is about creating support for that intention for each of us.

It is also important that I don't equate success with my intention to be in solid, long-term recovery from sugar and food addiction with 100% abstinence. I don't know if 100% abstinence from compulsive overeating or sugar consumption is possible. I won't know until I've done it. I do know I can do abstinence for long periods of time. Where I get into trouble is when I relapse and then don't recommit to my intention, but instead move into food free-for-all for months and years. Instead of turning away, I want now to turn toward the problem, to turn back to my recovery.

The shift in focus must be on what we really want, not what we can't have. We can focus on food sobriety and the freedom from shame, guilt, misery. We can focus on feeling great and not on certain foods that we miss.

I've come to realize that if I'm not committed to my commitments, they aren't commitments. So every day now, I commit to no sugars, no flours, no snacks, appropriate quantities, and trusting that those quantities will be enough, that I can survive and thrive without consuming more.

FOOD FOR THOUGHT

199 What resistance comes up for you when you read these steps? How can you tame that resistance?

200 Make a list of things you want out of recovery from food addiction. Be as specific as you can.

201 What sustainable program of abstinence and healthy eating could you create or find?

203 Which of the ideas presented here resonate with you? Which can you implement to support your recovery?

204 What might constitute your circle of support? How might you enroll them in supporting you?

205 What are starting to show up for you as meaningful and satisfying activities?

206 How might you let go of the dream of an easier, softer way?

207 What specific plan can you develop for recommitting to recovery if you relapse?

TOOLS FOR CHANGE

Create your food sobriety list. How can you use this in your shopping and meal planning?

Find one meaningful, satisfying activity and make it a part of your life each day or at least each week.

I KNOW YOU CAN DO IT

208
WORKING YOUR PROGRAM SO IT WILL WORK FOR YOU

Recovery is an ongoing process. The 12 Steps call it *working your program*. Bright Line Eating calls it *automaticity*, having well-established habits around eating that keep us anchored in safety. The more times we say no to demon foods, the easier it becomes. The more times we weigh our food and eat exactly that, the more automatic it becomes.

Recovery can be hard work. If we're in weight loss, we'll most likely be hungry some of the time, something we've tried hard to avoid. We may be tired for a while as our body adjusts to the new food plan. We may get weary of eating differently than those around us, of having to ask for accommodations. It can seem much simpler to go back to eating anything and everything. But that won't get us what we want. Freedom from addiction. Freedom from obsession. Freedom from excess weight.

At 26 years sober, I still go to AA meetings, still read the literature, still use the tools I first learned to keep me sober from alcohol. It's insurance against relapse. I know my recovery from food addiction requires the same long-term commitment if I want the same long-term success. I know that losing all the weight I want is not recovery. Eating three sane and moderate meals a day without sugar, flour, or snacks—that's recovery. That's my commitment. Living into that commitment is how I work my program.

I was having lunch recently with a good friend. It was a delicious meal of steak, garlicky green beans, and fire-roasted veggies. I was really happy with my meal. I glanced over at the next table where a woman was sitting alone. She was eating some kind of chocolate cake with vanilla ice cream and it triggered a craving in me. I just really wanted that. I wasn't hungry. I wasn't dissatisfied. I just wanted that dessert.

I haven't had a lot of cravings since I stopped eating sugar and flour. I've been so relieved to be free of worry and fear and guilt that the thought of eating that stuff has made me kind of sick. But that day in the restaurant, I really wanted that cake and that ice cream. I knew how good it would taste.

And that's when I came to my senses. I knew exactly how it would taste because I had eaten something like it before. I had that memory. And after five minutes—that's all the time it would take me to eat it—I'd only have the memory again. So what would be different from the memory I have now? Nothing good. Just a bunch of sugar and fat and flour. Stronger cravings. A return to self-loathing. No thanks.

—From my journal

209
BECOMING AN EXCEPTION

Since the percentage of people in successful recovery from food is small (most studies show about 10% of those who enter recovery stay in it for the long term), clearly we must consider how to position ourselves to be one of those few, to be an exception. What do we need to find that they can't seem to find?

A lot of the ideas here address this. We have to find a real commitment to loving ourselves enough to put recovery first. We have to shift our narrow focus from always seeking enough of our demon foods in order to stay numb to creating a life that means so much to us, that satisfies us so deeply that the demon foods and being numb lose their appeal.

When I stopped drinking, I realized that I had to want to NOT drink more than I wanted to drink. Now I have to want to NOT eat sugar and flour and snacks more than I want to eat them. I can do this consciously, keeping my mind focused on my desire for peace of mind and the joys of a right-sized body. I can also do this less consciously by building strong neural pathways of recovery: eating right quantities of healthy food, staying out of drama and stress, being honest with my feelings.

We can practice saying no to things that don't serve our recovery and yes to things that do until it's automatic and easy. We can learn to be with discomfort, both cravings and feelings; when we struggle with that, we can seek and use support from friends, family, other addicts, and professionals.

We can thoroughly follow the path we've chosen for our recovery. Thoroughly following the path gives us hope for success. We can keep coming back to this moment where choice lies, the only moment where it does. Once we're mired in addictive eating, we have little choice any more. But choice is one of the great gifts of life and recovery gives it back to us.

Are you ready to be an exception? You can choose it today. You can start abstaining today. You can start creating your sweet and wonderful and exceptional life between meals right now.

CANDY GIRL

210
IS IT EVER TOO LATE TO RECOVER?

My simplest answer to this question is no. As long as we can feed ourselves and have choices about what we put in our mouths, we can recover from food addiction. We can say no to sugar and flour, we can choose to not eat between meals if that's a trigger, we can say no to other demon foods we've identified. We can be 95 and do this.

However, it may not be possible for all of us to lose all the weight we want and more possibly not as quickly as we want. Bodies differ in their ability to shed their stores of fat. It can take some people a year to lose 20 pounds while someone else loses 120 pounds in that same year even though they are eating the same foods and same quantities of those foods. Our individual responses vary as do our histories with food and dieting, and those histories can impact aspects of our recovery.

Can we all be thin? I don't know. Can we all be free of compulsive eating? Yes. We can take back control of what we eat and how we care for our bodies. It will take all those things I've been taking about: courage, persistence, help from others, changing major and minor ways we live, finding a path that works for us, often through trial and error. But it is so worth it.

Two Last Questions

- How much more misery do you need before you join me?
- What one action, no matter how small, could you take today towards creating a wonderful life between meals?

There is life after sugar, a very sweet life. I hope you can put down your fork and create that life for yourself. Let me know how I can support you in doing that.

At-a-Glance
210 WAYS TO CREATE A SWEETER LIFE BETWEEN MEALS

PART I: THE WAY IN

HOW I FELL INTO SUGAR AND FOOD ADDICTION
1. I'm addicted to sugar
2. Three experiences that set me up for self-medicating with food
3. Enter sugar, enter addiction
4. Addiction and anxiety
5. Sugar and my early recovery from alcoholism
6. Sugar and getting fat
7. My adventures in dieting, Part I
8. What sugar addiction looked like on me

Poem: *When I'm in relapse*

9. My adventures in dieting, Part II
10. Giving up sugar again and again
11. Dealing with my own entrenched resistance
12. What I still needed to sort out

Poem: *When relapse stops working*

IS SUGAR ADDICTION REAL?
13. A little about research on sugar and addiction
14. A bit more about research
15. How much proof do we need that we suffer?
16. Addiction makes us irrational
17. Are you a sugar or food addict?
18. The hard work of the addict

BREAKING FREE
19. Why I think most diets don't work
20. The most important reason diets don't work
21. What it takes to break free
22. Saying it and accepting it are not the same thing
23. It takes what it takes to be willing
24. We aren't ready until we're ready

THE WAY OUT

THE OBSTACLES TO OVERCOME

25 Creating an environment for change
26 Changing my environment helped me let go of food as a crutch
27 Self-sabotage: Entitlements
28 Self-sabotage: Justifications
29 Self-sabotage: Excuses
30 Recognizing and shifting our self-sabotage
31 Recovery helps us change our relationship with the past
32 Getting out of the self-sabotage loop
33 Unconscious sabotage from friends
34 Unconscious sabotage from family
35 Health professionals may not be help professionals
36 Some reasons health professionals may not be so helpful
37 Cultural sabotage: Food for profit
38 More on food for profit
39 Food addiction and the TV
40 Living in a culture obsessed with thin
41 And then there are the holiday landmines
42 Environmental sabotage

HOW SOOTHING OURSELVES IS THE REAL PROBLEM

43 The paradox of taking care of ourselves
44 When the solution becomes the problem
45 Stress and trauma are my problem, not food
46 My version of food insecurity
47 Eating to soothe ourselves
48 Eating to escape hyper-vigilance
49 Eating to belong
50 Eating and the inner child
51 Giving ourselves attention rather than food
52 Then there's shame
53 And the fear of happiness

PART II: THE WAY OUT

WE COMMIT TO CHANGING OUR STORIES
54 How our stories get us into trouble and how they can save us
55 Finding the courage to give up old defense mechanisms
56 Curiosity is one of our most important tools
57 Worthiness doesn't have prerequisites
58 The importance of changing our stories
59 Changing our lives helps us change our stories
60 Some ways to change our stories
61 Changing our way of thinking about food

WE COMMIT TO GROWING UP
62 In recovery, we choose to grow up
63 Growing up and dealing with negative emotions
64 Recovery means taking responsibility for our lives—and our bodies
65 Accepting the right kind of responsibility

WE COMMIT TO CHANGING OUR BRAINS
66 What triggers us
67 Cravings: How they work and how to manage them
68 Cravings and playing out the tape
69 Other kinds of triggers
70 My old brain groove
71 Creating a new brain groove
72 Taking advantage of our brain's ability to change
73 Perhaps the most important thing to practice
74 The benefits of my practice
75 The role of habits in food addiction
76 Some good suggestions for building better habits
77 Change takes time
78 Readjust if you return to the old behavior: Face it, admit it, start again

WE COMMIT TO MANAGING OUR STRESSES
79 The life that supports our active addiction may not support our recovery
80 Stress and recovery from food addiction

81 Stress and the willpower gap
82 Changing how we deal with stress in our work
83 Dealing with financial stress
84 Group support for alleviating financial stress
85 Doing what we can to alleviate relationship stresses
86 Health stresses
87 The stress of pretending to be normal
88 We usually need to go slow and make incremental changes
89 Identify your stresses
90 Create an action plan for alleviating a major stressor
91 Choosing peace over drama
92 Get help for tough decisions
93 Take responsibility for your success

WE COMMIT TO ABSTINENCE IN ONE FORM OR ANOTHER
94 What is abstinence?
95 I had to surrender to abstinence
96 Moving away from abstinence as punishment
97 Adopting abstinence as a helpful attitude
98 Abstinence for me means no snacks
99 Does abstinence mean I have to do it perfectly?
100 What about relapse

WE COMMIT TO CHANGING OUR LIVES
101 Moving out of stuck into satisfaction
102 The need for a structured life
103 Why we have to change how we eat as well as what we eat
104 Building a 3-meal life
105 More on how I've changed my food life
106 Creating a meaningful life between meals supports recovery
107 Creating a deeply satisfying life supports recovery
108 More about meaning and satisfaction in recovery
109 Why the meaningful is so important to my recovery
110 Some of what works for me
111 Planning for the meaningful
112 Some of how I keep the meaningful front and center in my recovery

WE COMMIT TO CHANGING OUR RELATIONSHIP WITH FOOD

113 We can take charge of our food
114 We can eat well even with minimal cooking
115 A word about BLTs
116 We can make sure we have delicious food
117 Changing my definition of *delicious*
118 We can make everything we eat something good for our bodies
119 We can eat only food, not treats
120 We can learn to celebrate without food
121 We can food-proof our home
122 Eating automatically is not eating unconsciously
123 The value of committing our food
124 The recovery program I subscribe to
125 What I eat
126 Bright lines as a way to imagine our commitment to recovery
127 Food allergies, health issues, and individual triggers
128 Hunger and food-tripping
129 On choosing not to live life waiting for the next meal
130 Handling tough food situations

WE COMMIT TO CHANGING OUR RELATIONSHIP WITH OURSELVES

131 Accepting that we have an illness
132 It can be helpful to admit our powerlessness over food
133 Accepting that change is hard
134 Protecting ourselves emotionally
135 Avoiding becoming too tired, lonely, or angry
136 Dealing with tired: Resting and paring back on our schedule
137 Ideas for more and better rest
138 Addressing our loneliness
139 What about anger?
140 Dealing with positive emotions
141 Being in and returning to the moment
142 Recovery means showing up for life
143 The value and difficulty of goals
144 The freedom we can feel when weight loss is a secondary goal
145 The courage to be uncomfortable

146 Finally learning to love our bodies
147 Forgiving ourselves, loving ourselves
148 We can learn to trust by telling the truth
149 We can be willing to stay conscious
150 We can come to grips with the four F's
151 Analysis is usually of little help
152 We can find support to do nothing
153 We can live from curiosity and discovery
154 Discipline vs. commitment and the need for community

WE CAN'T GO IT ALONE
155 Creating a community of support
156 More on creating a support system
157 Getting a grip on the 50-pound phone
158 Support from AA, OA, or other food issue groups
159 Abstinence and recovery as service
160 Helping others can help us

Poem: *My food addiction is not just about me*

TOOLS WE CAN USE TO SUPPORT OUR RECOVERY
161 Creating a list of soothers
162 More thoughts on soothers
163 16 Solutions is a helpful brainstorming tool
164 Daily journaling for recovery
165 Using meditation to strengthen our recovery
166 Central column breathing
167 Avoiding mindlessness or "keep coming back"
168 Embracing the importance of exercise
169 For some of us, the free ride is over
170 Giving up our excuses so we can live well
171 It's never too late to start exercising
172 However, take it slow and easy during weight loss
173 A helpful book and a great exercise
174 Getting started on your own exercise program
175 Weight training can help you look better naked
176 What my activity plan looks like

USING CREATIVITY FOR A STRONGER RECOVERY
177   How I found my creative self
178   Putting our natural abilities to work for our recovery
179   How creative self-expression can support our recovery
180   10 ways to get started as a creative

OTHER WAYS OF TAKING CARE OF OURSELVES
181   Offering unconditional friendliness to ourselves
182   Creating a circle of well-being
183   Creating a rest practice
184   Using or not using the scale
185   A word about being weighed at the doctor's

Poem: *On finally owning my body as it is*

WE COMMIT TO BEING IN RECOVERY FOR THE LONG HAUL
186   Organizing our inner lives
187   The possibility of relapse
188   Life works best with rigorous honesty
189   The spiritual part of the journey
190   Increasing my conscious contact
191   Consider using prayer and ritual
192   "Thoroughly followed our path"
193   Moving from discipline to devotion
194   Expanding our repertoire of pleasures
195   Lightening up how we live
196   Thriving or surviving?
197   Stepping into choice: Creating our lives in every moment
198   Easing the uncertainty of life with our food plan

CREATING THE LIFE BETWEEN MEALS
199   Suggested steps for enhancing successful recovery from food addiction
200   Clearly understanding what we want from recovery
201   Adopting and maintaining a sustainable plan of abstinence and healthy eating
202   Embracing food sobriety

203 Developing habits that support our well-being
204 Creating a circle of support with others who suffer from food addiction
205 Creating a meaningful and satisfying life between meals
206 Letting go of our search for the easier, softer way
207 Making an unwavering commitment to recommit to recovery

I KNOW YOU CAN DO IT
208 Working your program so it will work for you
209 Becoming an exception
210 Is it ever too late to recover?

Resources

Sober Play: Using Creativity for a More Joyful Recovery by Jill Kelly. Available on amazon and from the author: **www.jillkellyauthor.com**

Sober Truths: The Making of an Honest Woman by Jill Kelly. Available on amazon and from the author: **www.jillkellyauthor.com**

The Artist's Way by Julia Cameron

www.brightlineeating.com

Overeaters Anonymous: **www.oa.org** for a meeting near you

"Cravings" by Doug Lisle, PHD. **http://www.forksoverknives.com/cravings-how-they-work-and-how-to-manage-them/**

The End of Overeating by David Kessler, MD.

Fat Chance by Robert Lustig, MD.

Fat, Sick, and Nearly Dead (free on youtube)

Forks over Knives (documentary)

The Life-Changing Magic of Tidying Up by Marie Kondo.

Real Fitness for Real Women by Rochelle Rice. **www.rochellerice.com**

Spiritual Advantages of a Painful Childhood by Wayne Muller

That Sugar Film (documentary)

Any of the writings of Michael Pollan, including http://www.nytimes.com/2013/05/19/magazine/say-hello-to-the-100-trillion-bacteria-that-make-up-your-microbiome.html?pagewanted=8&_r=3&ref=michaelpollan

A most moving letter on diet, food, body image, and the industry that fuels it. **(http://www.huffingtonpost.com/iris-higgins/an-open-apology-to-all-of_b_3762714.html)**

An articulate statement on food, health, and business **(http://opinionator.blogs.nytimes.com/2013/08/06/11-trillion-reasons/?emc=eta1&_r=1)**

The milkshake study **(http://ajcn.nutrition.org/content/early/2013/06/26/ajcn.113.064113.abstract)**

More about cravings **http://www.balancedweightmanagement.com/Understand%20Brain%20Chemistry%20and%20Weight.htm**

The Life Between Meals Program

Visit **www.lifebetweenmealscoaching.com** for more information and tools on how you can give up sugar and food addiction and create a great life between meals.

You'll find information about how to:

- Sign up for an online course in creating your life between meals.
- Invite me to lead a workshop or speak to your group or conference.
- Download the quiz, the eating plan, and other free tools.
- Connect with others on the *Life between Meals* path.
- Order *Sober Play: Using Creativity for a More Joyful Recovery*.
- Join the mailing list.

Acknowledgements

Enormous gratitude to all those who have encouraged me in my recovery but especially to Lily Gael, Anna Petros, Susan Brooks, Pamela Stringer, Meredith Gunter, Carole Warner, NutriBob Wilson, Shannon Kelly, Kerry Kelly, Melanie St John, and my BLE friends, Annie Britton, Carolyn Shipley, Heidi Snyder, and Janet Brandt. A special thank-you to Susan Peirce Thompson whose Bright Line program finally showed me the way home.

About the Author

Jill Kelly, PhD, is an author, editor, painter, and coach. She has been in recovery from addiction since 1989. She lives in Portland, Oregon, with her four cats.

To sign up for my blog:
www.sobertruths.blogspot.com

To find about my books:
www.jillkellyauthor.com

To find about my art or sign up for my creativity newsletter:
www.jillkellycreative.com

Connect with me at
jill@lifebetweenmealscoaching.com.